Changed Identities

Changed Identities

The Challenge of the New Generation in Saudi Arabia

Mai Yamani

THE ROYAL INSTITUTE OF
INTERNATIONAL AFFAIRS
Middle East Programme

© Royal Institute of International Affairs, 2000

First published in Great Britain in 2000 by
Royal Institute of International Affairs, 10 St James's Square,
London SW1Y 4LE
(Charity Registration No. 208 223)

HN766
.A8
M35
2000x

Distributed worldwide by
The Brookings Institution, 1775 Massachusetts Avenue NW,
Washington DC 20036-2188, USA

British Library Cataloguing in Publication Data
A CIP catalogue record for this book is available from the British Library.

ISBN 1 86203 088 X

Typeset in Times by Koinonia
Printed and bound in Great Britain by the Chameleon Press
Cover illustration by Gillian Golding

'In one generation we went from riding camels
to riding Cadillacs. The way we are wasting money,
I fear the next generation will be riding camels again.'

The late King Faisal
Ruler of Saudi Arabia, 1965–75

Contents

Contents

About the author

Dr Mai Yamani studied for her BA in anthropology at Bryn Mawr College, Pennsylvania before going up to Somerville College, Oxford for her Master's degree in social anthropology. Thereafter, she gained her doctorate from Oxford University.

In 1981, she was appointed lecturer in social anthropology and sociology at the King Abdul Aziz University, Jeddah. Subsequently she has been a Research Fellow at the Centre for Cross-Cultural Research on Women at Oxford and Academic Adviser to the Center for Contemporary Arab Studies at Georgetown University, Washington, DC. She is a research associate at the Centre of Islamic and Middle Eastern Law at the School of Oriental and African Studies (SOAS), University of London, and a Research Fellow with the Middle East Programme at the Royal Institute of International Affairs.

Dr Yamani has lectured extensively in Britain, the United States and the Middle East on social, economic, cultural and human rights issues in Arab states, particularly the Gulf Cooperation Council states, and has broadcast widely on these subjects internationally on both television and radio. In addition to her academic publications, she has written columns and features on social affairs for Arabic newspapers.

Acknowledgments

I should like to express my thanks to a number of people, whose support and encouragement have been invaluable in the realization of this work. The idea for the project leading to this book was conceived in 1997 in discussions with Dr Rosemary Hollis, Head of the Middle East Programme at Chatham House. Not only did she help in brainstorming the themes, but she buoyed the project along with her endless energy. I should like to acknowledge the financial support of the sponsors of the Middle East Programme who made this project possible.

My thanks to those scholars who gave their professional views of the work as it progressed, in particular Professor Gregory Gause and Dr Mustafa Alani. Toby Dodge, of the School of Oriental and African Studies and my colleague at Chatham House, has lent a very sympathetic ear and contributed by challenging my ideas and approach. I am grateful to Raksha Thakor, for the work she put in on repeated retyping of the manuscript and her administrative efficiency throughout. Talal Fandi, my research assistant in the initial stage of the project, helped with identifying secondary source material, and later with organizing the fieldwork material. Finally, I should like to thank Margaret May, Head of the Publications Department at Chatham House, and Dr Kim Mitchell for applying their sharp and meticulous eyes to the text before it went to press.

My greatest debt is to the Saudi youth, who offered their trust and cooperation during lengthy interviews. As I promised each one of them, they shall remain absolutely anonymous. Two very special young people can be named, however – my daughters Zain and Fatima, who gave me access to the world of youth, even though they were not interviewed. The book belongs to the young Saudis and I hope I have succeeded in delivering their message faithfully, but needless to say, I bear the responsibility for the end product, warts and all.

April 2000   M.Y.

Glossary

'abaya	woman's black cloak
abu 'iyal	a man with children to support
adabi	the arts
ahl al-hal wal-'aqd	those who bind and loose
al-hay'a	'The Committee' (for the propagation of good and the forbidding of evil)
al-jam'iyya al-faysaliyya	Faisal's (charitable) Organization
al-jam'iyya al-khayriyya	The Charitable Organization
al-khidma al-madaniyya	civil service
al-tanzeem	organization
'amal	witchcraft
arbita	charity housing for abandoned women
ashiqaa'	full brothers
'ashura	the Shi'a annual mourning for the death of Hussein
ayyam al-sahaba	the era of the Prophet's companions
'azayim	feasts
ba'zagha	waste
bid'a	innovation in religion
bidun ghalat	without sinning
bint an-nas	the daughter of good people
dar al-hanan	House of Tenderness
dawla	central government
falah	success
fatwa	religious edict
fihm	understanding
fiqh	Islamic jurisprudence
fitna	provocation leading to chaos
ghara	raid
ghasb	force-feeding
ghazal	romantic flattery
hadith	the sayings of the prophet Muhammad
halal	religiously approved
hanafi	Islamic school of law following the teachings of imam Abu Hanifa
hanbali	Islamic school of law following the teachings of imam Ahmed bin Hanbal
haram	religiously forbidden
haram aleikum	have mercy on him
hasad	'the evil eye'

hashu	stuffing
hijab	women's veil
hukuma	central government
'ibada	worship
ibtida'i	elementary
i'dadi	secondary
ihtiram	respect
ijma'	consensus
iltizam	obligation
'ilmi	sciences
iman	faith
inshallah, bukra, maleish	Allah willing, tomorrow, it is all right
'isma	the right to obtain a divorce based on preset conditions in the marriage contract
ittikali	rentier mentality
juhalla	ignorant
kalam an-nas	people's gossip
katma	suffocation
kuttab	school for the memorization and study of the Quran
lazem	a must
mahr	dowry offered by the groom to the bride
majlis	regular gathering for discussions
majlis al-shura	consultative council
maliki	Islamic school of law following the teaching of imam Malik
mashaikh	religious authorities
mawlid	the ceremony of the birth of the Prophet Muhammad
mazahir	appearances
mihrim	male relative whom a woman is forbidden to marry
mu'akasa	intrusion (by a male towards a female)
muhajjaba	practice whereby women cover the body and hair, except for face and hands
mulhi	a distraction from the faith
munharifin	idiosyncratic
mustawa	socio-economic level
mutafatiha	open-minded
mutaw'a	members of the Committee for the Propagation of Good and the Forbidding of Evil (religious police)
mutawwifin	guides for the pilgrims
nafaqa	divorce/separation settlement according to Islamic law
namati	set in his ways
nazariiya	theory
qadar	fate
rashwa	bribe
rawdat al ma'aref	The Garden of Knowledge

Glossary

riba	forbidden financial interest
rida	contentment
riyadh al atfal	The Oasis of Children
rizq	provisions
sadaqa	alms-giving
sah	correct
salafi	a wahhabi form of Islamic teachings
shafi'	Islamic school of law following the teachings of imam al Safi'i
shari'a	Islamic law
sheitan	the devil
shilla	peer grouping based on gender
shura	consultation in Islamic tradition
subhan-Allah	Allah's wonders
sulta	authority
tab'iyya	civil status card
tafra	boom
takhasusi	specialist government hospital
taw'ia	enlightenment
thoub	men's garment
'ulama	religious scholars
uli al-amr	those with authority
umara	princes or those with political authority
umma	Islamic nation
ummahat al mu'minin	'mothers of the believers'
wakil shar'i	man with power of attorney
wasta	family connections
yaum al-tahaddi	day of confrontation
zabiha	(eating) the whole lamb
zakat	Islamic tax system
zakat al-fitr	levy at the end of the month of Ramadan

Preface

Muhammad's story

My name is Muhammad. I am a Saudi. This is my story.

I was born in 1975 in the Saudi city of Jeddah, which lies on the coast of the Red Sea. I am the first-born of seven children: four girls and three boys. My father, Abdul Jalil, is a government employee; my mother, Maryam, a housewife. They both came from families that had known each other for generations and were linked by ties of marriage and kinship. My paternal grandparents, both of whom now live with my family in Jeddah, came originally from Bahra, a village lying between Mecca and Jeddah. They are first cousins. In his day, my grandfather used to teach the Quran at the local kuttab *(school for the memorization and study of the Quran) and the* hadith *(the sayings of the prophet Muhammad) in Bahra, and he was considered at the time to be highly knowledgeable. As for my grandmother, most of her life seems to have been preoccupied with the task of raising her eleven children. She had actually given birth to seventeen, but six died in infancy. She tells me this was quite normal in the old days.*

I completed both my primary and secondary education at a government school in Jeddah. I remember my school years as being easy: like all other Saudi students, I had everything provided for me: books, stationery and an allowance. It was all part of the generous welfare system provided by the government. The state took care of all our needs. We never had to worry about not having something we needed for school. However, this system has not continued. The days of plenty ended with the beginning of the recession in our economy. To make it worse, when I was fifteen the Gulf war broke out and our government spent a great deal of money buying arms to protect us from the enemy and to pay for the extravagant needs of the Americans.

At school, I studied 'ilmi *(sciences). My family always wanted me to become a doctor or an engineer. In fact, most people in Saudi Arabia think that it is a waste of time and effort to do anything else at university, especially if it is something in the arts. I also had no desire to study at one of the* shari'a *(Islamic law) colleges since I knew that this would not guarantee me a job. Too many people I know studied at Imam Saud University and are now unemployed. I knew for certain that I had no interest in becoming a* mutawi', *a member of the religious police, running around reprimanding people. Anyway, the requirements for a basic religious education were largely satisfied by what I had been taught during my primary and secondary schooling as well as the teachings I received at home. I have always prayed five times a day and lived my life according to the five pillars of Islam. Because of the fierce competition to enrol at the university, my father had to use the* wasta *(family connections) of his superiors at work in order to secure me a place at the medical school. Since I did not have the grade point average required for enrolment at university,* wasta *was crucial for me. And it worked. In fact, it always works out if you have the right connections.*

I did not like medical school. I was enrolled for two years before finally dropping out. I don't think my family was very happy with my decision to leave, but there was nothing much else I could have done. I then had to start searching for a job. I never thought it would be such a difficult task. I mean, in my father's days, things used to be so easy. There was always a job for you if you wanted one. There was also financial support from the government for anyone in need. But it seems things have changed since then. Now, there is a lot of talk about problems in the economy and that there is not as much money as there used to be in the old days. I find it difficult to comprehend, especially if you think about all that money generated from oil production. But I guess there are a lot of problems in the system: this is what everyone says. Anyway, I am not an economist and I never could fully grasp the logic of economics or finance.

After one year of frustration and disappointment, I finally succeeded in finding a job at a travel agent's office through a family friend. It was not exactly what I was dreaming of, but it was good enough. At first I enjoyed it. But soon it became increasingly difficult, especially because I had to compete with all the expatriate employees. This was very tough. They had one main advantage over me: they spoke very good English. The English I was taught at school was obviously not good enough. Eventually, I had to leave my job because I fell out with my boss. He said I was a liability: not only did I not have the necessary English skills, but he also thought my 'work ethic' was not acceptable. I never understood what he meant by that. In any case, it was clear that he wanted to hire another expatriate since it's much cheaper for him than having a Saudi. I understood that I was fired and so I left.

During the few months I had worked at the travel agent's, I managed to save some money, and together with the round trip ticket (Jeddah/Cairo/London/Jeddah) I was given, I decided to embark on my first tour outside Saudi Arabia. I was then twenty-one years old. Together with my close friends from school, Abdul Rahman, Abdullah and Wael, I visited Cairo. Though several of my friends had been there before, and had gone on and on about the place and how much they loved it, I was still not prepared at all for what I saw. Though I had heard people before talking about culture shock, I was not sure I understood exactly what they were referring to, and even then, I certainly never thought I would experience a culture shock in another Arab Muslim country. It was completely unlike anything I had expected or seen, despite the fact that I have seen many strange things alien to our culture on satellite television. For the first time in my life, I felt extremely uneasy about myself: many of the things that formed the core of my belief system and outlook on life were suddenly being challenged. What I found most disturbing was being so challenged in a Muslim country with an Arab culture. Unlike in Saudi Arabia, where it is inconceivable that a woman would expose herself in public places, in Egypt unveiled women were all over the place. It was fascinating. What I found even more shocking was that both males and females were allowed to mingle freely. And they had cinemas and night clubs. There were no mutaw'a to admonish them! I had always thought that the mutaw'a were part and parcel of every Islamic state.

In the open, in tea and coffee houses, we saw Egyptians openly discussing and debating political issues. It had never occurred to me before that ordinary people need to discuss such issues among themselves. I mean, if they are not the ones who are ruling the country, why should they bother themselves with such issues? What impact would they have? I was horrified to hear them express their negative opinions of their leaders. In Saudi Arabia, we never do this. I am still not sure what I think about it all, but such provocative behaviour (fitna) could lead to chaos.

In London I found an even more open and free environment, with many more strange things awaiting me. I knew it was part of a different world, *alien to us Saudis. With my friends, we gathered around Arab places in which, luckily for us, people not only spoke our native Arabic language but offered* halal *(religiously approved) food. We bought our own newspapers and, surprisingly, heard political debates among different Arabs and between our own countrymen. We encountered many publications that attacked the system and government in Saudi Arabia. What was most shocking was that some of these publications were written by Saudis. One of my friends – I don't want to mention his name – was constantly buying and reading controversial publications. I worried for all our sakes that we might get caught and punished if his actions were discovered.*

For the first time, it struck me that we live in a very big world with many opportunities and many things to see. Exciting as it may have been, it nonetheless was utterly confusing. Before, I always had the impression that the world actually revolved around Islam and around our society. In London, I was intimidated and overwhelmed by the diversity and freedom of expression. For the first time, I felt the need and urge to go back to my country and be with my family, who had by then already assigned me a bride.

My mother had very good taste when she chose Reem to be my wife. Not only is she fair but she is endowed with beautiful Arab looks. Reem is five years my junior, a perfect age. In fact, my family had to offer a high mahr *(bride-price) and borrowed money to meet the sum. However, my mother did not foresee the difficult character Reem had. On the one hand, she is adamant about pursuing her university education; yet on the other hand, she is not quite sure what career path she intends to follow, since she says that the authorities place too many restrictions on the choices women can make. Similarly, while politely entertaining my family's demands for us to have children, she is not willing to oblige at this point in time.*

Eventually Allah answered my mother's prayers when I was selected from a big pool of applicants to be employed by a renowned British engineering company. The job involved a full-year training programme in Riyadh followed by six months in Britain. I finally found security through professional specialization – even though you don't make as much money as people used to do in the days of plenty, you still have respectability. The British are not as generous or lively as the Americans but they are reliable.

In Riyadh, I have to deal with many Englishmen and their rules, working from nine to five with no mercy, without even a break for a proper lunch or siesta. In addition, Riyadh has an isolating, rigid and sombre life-style compared to Jeddah. But we are entertained every evening via satellite television made available in the compound. And everything is available on these channels! American movies and songs, Arabic channels from Egypt, Lebanon and the MBC, as well as controversial but popular political programmes on Al Jazira Television from Qatar.

I find this all very enriching. My English-language skills have improved dramatically. My job prospects seem better than those of many others of my generation. However, with all the bombardment of satellite television, the English-language advertising, the pizza and hamburger and other fast-food chains, I sometimes wish that I could live in my grandfather's village, where life was traditional and secure. People trusted their neighbours and helped one another. There was genuine generosity and strong moral values. But alas! Even the village has now changed. Nothing remains of it but that which is relayed to me through my grandfather's nostalgia. The good things that were associated with our parents' generation seem to be no longer within our grasp. They had a stable life with financial security and strong family bonds. The government was able to take care of us all; but now, whether the government has less money or there are too many of us, or it just doesn't care about our welfare, I cannot understand, but it is about time we started changing things for ourselves.

I remain an optimist. This situation and all this struggle cannot be in vain. I am going to persevere. Ideas are brewing in my head. Together with my friends, soon we will find a way of moving forward.

* * *

Muhammad is a composite construction who represents the beliefs, aspirations, ambitions, frustrations and fears of the large and complex social grouping which is the new generation. Muhammad has many 'brothers and sisters', all members of Saudi Arabia's new generation. Not all of them have his attitudes and inclinations, but they do have the same fears and preoccupations. Their perceptions of the socio-economic changes facing Saudi Arabia are shaped by similar experiences and socialization processes. Muhammad represents the average response, the middle of the range of the broad spectrum of young people interviewed. Their voices and opinions will be expressed throughout this book in their own words.

The centrality of the new generation

The centrality of 15–30-year-olds to the future of Saudi Arabia is hard to underestimate; their numbers alone make them the crucial political constituency of the next ten years. The most conservative estimates put more than 50 per cent of the population below the age of 20 and only 17.2 per cent above the age of 40.[1] The Gulf Cooperation Council (GCC) estimates that the number of Saudis and expatriates under 15 is 33.6 per cent of the whole population. This translates to 40.9 per cent of the purely Saudi population. If these estimates approximate the truth, even the most conservative figures demonstrate the very high proportion of Saudis who are still under, but rapidly approaching, working age.[2]

Saudi Arabia, like other countries in the GCC, is facing the major problem of finding ways to absorb its youth into the labour force while containing expectations for wider political participation. At a time when private investment is levelling off, oil revenues are unstable, and massive public spending exceeds revenues, Saudis are bewildered as to how they can manage this expanding population, a decreasing mortality rate as well as an increasing demand for female employment.[3]

Currently, around 3.5 million Saudis (approximately 27 per cent of the population) are in schools, colleges and universities.[4] In the year 2000, an estimated 660,000 Saudi nationals are expected to join the labour market.[5]

---

[1] *The GCC Economic Databook*, 1996, p. 95.

[2] In 1974, the official census estimated the Saudi population to be 6,218,381. The 1992 census, however, put it at 12.3 million. The virtual doubling of official Saudi population figures in 18 years necessitates that all official figures be treated with scepticism. Currently, government figures estimate the population to be approximately 18 million, including foreign workers and their families, who are officially estimated to form 29 per cent of the total population. The United Nations estimated that the population of Saudi Arabia in 1975 was 7,251,000, rising to 8,9600,00 by 1980. This tendency for official statistics to overestimate the population has serious implications for any demographic analysis, especially of the anticipated extent and effects of unemployment.

[3] NCB Economist, 'Gulf Population and Labour Force Structure', economic and financial publication issued by the Economics Department of the National Commercial Bank, Vol. 5, No. 4, June–July 1995, p. 3.

[4] Ibid., p. 5.

[5] Ibid., p. 3.

Understandable government concern about this situation is driven by a combination of a declining standard of living and an annual population growth rate of 3.3 per cent between 1992 and 2000. This means that an average of 125,000 Saudis enter an already contracting job market each year.[6] Examples from across the developing world, specifically from North Africa, have indicated that the spectre of political instability haunts regimes which fail to provide for the economic needs and social expectations of a youthful and expanding population.

Given the potential influence of the new generation across the GCC states and specifically in Saudi Arabia, this book describes their views, their hopes and their fears. It assesses the political implications of the rapid economic and social changes that Saudi Arabia has experienced over recent decades and their impact on the new generation. In interviewing a broad cross-section of young people from the Kingdom, I aim in this book to let them explain their situation in their own words.

The book has been structured around the broad themes that surfaced in the interviews, the themes that most concern the new generation today. The outstanding motif that united all the concerns and aspirations of the young people was the clash between continuity and change. The rapid oil-driven social transformation that Saudi Arabia has undergone in the space of two generations has deeply influenced the youth of the country. On one side they have the stabilizing and apparently constant influences of family and religion. In the rapidly changing global setting these provide certainty in an increasingly uncertain world. But this certainty comes at a cost. Those interviewed expressed considerable frustration with what they see as the constraining and negative aspects of continuity. No one among those interviewed expressed a desire to be outside the extended family structure or Islam but a majority did want to be given a greater degree of autonomy to define the parameters of their own morality.

The aspects of change that are welcomed by the new generation are those brought about by the technologies of globalization, satellite television and the Internet. For the youth these bring different cultures flooding into their lives. The youth deploy the perceived certainties of their parents' and grandparents' generations to interact with the polyglot culture they encounter with a large degree of confidence. But in the process they expand their horizons, and this has prompted widespread

[6] The World Bank, *World Tables 1994* (Baltimore/London: Johns Hopkins University, 1994).

discontent with the Saudi education system. Increasingly aware of what is available beyond the borders of the state, and finding themselves in direct competition with foreign workers in the Kingdom itself, young people are pressing for the modernization of the education system and the secularization of their curricula.

All these concerns have to be placed within the context of economic insecurity. The young people interviewed see that the support they can expect from the state is much less than their parents received. A growing realization that they will have to be self-sufficient as adults has produced a sense of insecurity but also a new spirit of questioning. The governing elite does not get automatic respect from a generation well aware of the excesses of the 1970s and 1980s. Stories of corruption and nepotism are common and believed. The reaction is a call for transparency and equality of access to government resources.

Overall this generation is not revolutionary and may not be mobilized by calls for radical political change. But to gain their quiescence they will have to be accommodated both socially and economically. This means listening to what the new generation has to say and allowing the Saudi education system and society to evolve to meet its needs.

1 Saudi identity: negotiating between tradition and modernity

Since its creation in 1932 Saudi Arabia has undergone rapid and continuous social, economic and cultural transformation. The three generations of the population that have lived under the rule of a specifically Saudi state have seen every aspect of their lives touched by the development of a unified state and the integration of that state into the world economy. What makes the new generation different is its size and potential influence. In order for Saudi Arabia to continue to prosper as a stable state the majority of the population that the new generation represents feel that they must be given jobs but also demand the social and political space to express their hopes and fears about the situation in which they find themselves.

This new generation perceives itself to be located between the institutions of the previous generation, most conspicuously those it views as 'traditional' – the family and religion – and the newer, modern institutions of the market and state. It is the members of the new generation who, like their parents and grandparents, will go on to re-examine just what is considered 'traditional' and 'modern'. It is they who will redefine the role of religion within a society that cannot avoid the gathering economic and social forces of a globalized world. Their views of the world they inhabit show that notions of tradition and modernity have become contested, with no single definition having common currency. The future of Saudi Arabia will, to a large degree, be decided by which of the competing definitions will triumph and guide the population as they reshape their lives and their relationship to the state.

The perceptions and attitudes of the new generation have been formed by an engagement with a wider range of possibilities than was available in recent times: travel for both work and leisure, education at home and abroad, a broad array of technological consumer goods, print and

1

electronic media. Many of those interviewed for this study experienced struggles with their family or the state over access to these possibilities, as a result of which they developed an acute awareness of the conflicting social and political interpretations among Saudis. There is, however, virtual unanimity over the characterization of the global market-place as the bearer of modernity and of the communities to which they belong as traditional. Modern life is frequently associated, for good or ill, with the West in general and specifically with the United States of America.

For most of those at the heart of this study, there is a sense of inevitability about the growth of the modern in their lives. Problems arise from the need to negotiate between the 'traditional' Saudi social basis to their lives and the modern pressures seen as emanating from outside. Pre-existing cultural identities seem less and less able to encompass the kinds of social practices and social relations to which the state and market have increasingly given rise. The task facing the new generation is the need to negotiate a sense of self in these new and unfamiliar circumstances. All the new generation, indeed all members of Saudi society, irrespective of their political and social affiliations, face the problems that modernity throws up. But depending on their understanding of the negative and positive effects of such interaction, their responses vary greatly. Under these conditions, cultural identities tend to range across a spectrum of positions from what could be called conservative or insular to liberal or eclectic. Whether conservative or liberal, cautious or expansive, insular or cosmopolitan, almost all express some ambivalence and a hybrid of complex reactions, attitudes and evaluations.

For 'conservatives', the new activities should, whenever possible, be subordinated to a moral sensibility more in keeping with tradition. These new activities should be encompassed by existing familial and religious institutions and they should be subject to higher authorities, including the state where appropriate. Those at the conservative or more cautious end of the spectrum also tend to see a pattern of moral decay spreading through society and are pessimistic about the effects of expanded market opportunities. They tend to promote traditional institutions as places from which people can acquire the traditionally based wisdom that will enable them to judge adequately the character of the opportunities provided by the market.

Those identified by their opinions as occupying the middle ground avoid proscribing social practices and shift towards a dilution of moral precepts so that their emerging conceptions of the good life encompass an ever widening range of novel activities. The largest constituency may be termed the 'pragmatists', those who through exposure to outside education and travel see the need for social change and reforms but are aware of limitations and inefficiencies in implementing this process. They tend to settle for the present situation as they consider it preferable to the uncertainty of radical change. Fearing social upheaval, the pragmatists believe a balance must be maintained between innovation and tradition.

'Liberal' opinion attempts to marginalize the sphere of tradition and is more optimistic about the moral implications of the new opportunities. More inclined to use a language of individual achievement than a language of the moral community, liberal thinkers tend in this context to minimize the scope of identity reference to the group. Liberals are more open to change and are keener to join a global economy.

Despite the differences, however, there is broad acceptance that there should be some fairly high level of congruence between an idea of what it is to be Muslim and what it is to engage in modern practices and to live with modern technologies and consumer goods. In fact, some conception of what it means to lead a virtuous life and some appreciation of what it means to have standards by which the individual, others and communities might be judged are more or less explicit in all the evaluations made of contemporary life. Naturally, conservative opinion is more restrictive, usually expressing a stronger sense of the dangers of engagement with the modern and emphasizing the role of community. Liberal opinion tends towards more market-oriented and individualist assessments of status which will be judged in terms of the practical skills and efforts which make for success in the market. The standards by which moral status is to be judged, however, have clearly entered a period of intense debate. This contest is the terrain on which identities of the new generation in Saudi Arabia are negotiated and reinvented.

The evolution of Saudi society: the story of the three generations

The best way to portray the extent to which society and the cultural references of ordinary Saudi Arabians have been transformed is by taking an 'ideal type', in this case the life experiences of a typical Saudi family. This family would have lived through the major landmarks of Saudi Arabia's twentieth-century history, the establishment of national unity, the oil era and globalization. The effects of modernization can best be judged by looking at a family in which the grandparents would have been born in the 1930s, the parents in the 1950s, and the new generation, the central focus of this book, in the 1970s and 1980s. The story of such a family can explain the evolving cultural identity and political consciousness against the backdrop of changing economic and political circumstances. Over a period of some sixty years the horizons of each successive generation have expanded, from the purely local to those bounded by the state and then to the present generation whose horizons are global.

The grandparents of this archetypal family would have been born in a decade of great historical significance for the Kingdom, namely that of political unification in 1932. The area that is now Saudi Arabia, prior to unification, encompassed separate territories with distinct political heritages: the southern region, Asir; the central region, Nejd; the eastern province, Ahsa; and the western region, the Hijaz. Before unification, the Hijaz had three schools of Islamic law: the *shafi'*, following the teachings of imam al-Safi'i; the *hanafi,* following the teachings of imam Abu Hanifa; and the *maliki,* following the teaching of imam Malik; while the Nejd had the *hanbali* school of law, following the teachings of imam Ahmed bin Hanbal, and specifically its interpretation by the wahhabi *'ulama* (religious scholars).[1]

The unification was a period of upheaval marked by civil war, especially between the Kingdom of Hijaz and the Sultanate of Nejd, and the assertion of a distinctive religious ideology, wahhabism. During the

[1] Wahhabism is a particular interpretation of the *hanbali* Islamic school of law, founded by Muhammad bin Abdul Wahhab (1703–87). Wahhabis, who prefer to call themselves Muwahhidun, are strictly monotheistic. The aim of the founder of the movement was to abolish all innovations *(bid'a)* which came after the third Islamic century.

youth of the grandparents, the peninsula was mostly a vast desert of largely nomadic rural communities. Identity (except for the populations of Mecca and Medina) was based on the family or tribe. Regional belonging was the basis of political identity, with variation of dialect, social behaviour, religious rituals, cuisine and dress. The grandfather wore his locally specific dress and the grandmother her distinctive clothes and jewellery. These and their dialect would have identified their origins. They also had a distinctive cuisine reflecting the physical environment and access to trading routes. As far as macro-political allegiances were concerned, the transition that the central government sought, from loyalties based on a tribal and/or regional identity to a national one, did not impact on the daily existence of the vast majority of the population. National homogeneity was certainly the objective of the newly established government under the Al-Saud family but this goal was unrealized in the 1930s and 1940s. The founder of the Kingdom, Abdul Aziz Al-Saud, aimed at a gradual integration and political unification, knowing that the gap between the regions was too wide to be bridged in a short time or by military coercion. The first vehicle of unification was wahhabi hanbalism as the official Saudi dogma.

The practical (as opposed to religious) horizons of the grandparents' imagination did not extend beyond the boundaries of their home town or village.[2] The grandfather's only means of transport was on foot or camel and later by truck; extended journeys were usually undertaken only once in a lifetime, and then to Mecca for pilgrimage. This reflected the economic circumstances of the time, characteristic of a country with almost negligible or as yet untapped resources, with the only major source of external income deriving from pilgrimage. Subsistence farming was dominant, with life organized around the scarcity of water. Villages outside main trading centres and ports were feebly connected to the areas surrounding them, let alone to the world economy. Trade was limited to the ports of Jeddah and those in the Ahsa. As far as education was concerned, the grandfather's knowledge did not go beyond religious education at the *kuttab* (schools for the memorization and study of the Quran) as well as tribal and local affairs. In modern terminology, one

---

[2] For a theoretical explanation of this argument in the European context, see Benedict Anderson, *Imagined Communities: Reflections on the Origins and Spread of Nationalism* (New York/London: Verso, 1991), especially Chapter 2.

would describe him as semi-literate. The exception was Hijaz, where there were more liberal educational centres, both in the great mosque of Mecca and in that of Medina, which accommodated diversity.[3]

The typical man of the grandfather's generation had one wife – unlike a minority of men who were better placed tribally and/or economically and had more. His wife was from the same lineage and more particularly the same extended family. The grandmother's major occupation in life was to produce and rear the offspring – an average of seven children, though the high infant mortality rate meant several others did not survive. The only help she had in raising her children were members of her extended family. Wealthier families may have also depended upon slaves to carry out domestic tasks.[4] The grandparents' generation came to adulthood when oil revenues had started to make their effects felt, but they still remembered pre-oil times. Oil brought non-Muslim foreigners to the newly established Saudi Arabia. The grandfather began to come into contact with non-Muslims for the first time in his life, particularly as American oil workers not only visited but started to have a quasi-permanent presence in the country.

The parents, those of the second generation, were born in the 1950s. They came to adulthood after the institutional structures of the state had been firmly established. National homogeneity became the norm with the unification of dress (all Saudi men adopted the national *thoub* and head-dress and all Saudi women the black *'abaya* in public), a national education curriculum and the beginnings of mass communication through the first national newspapers and radio. With these innovations it became possible to speak of the emergence of a Saudi Arabian identity. The process of integration became effective with the flow of oil revenues. Oil money accelerated the building of an infrastructure that in turn facilitated political integration. Travel throughout the Kingdom was commonplace. Saudis began to come into regular contact with and depend on state institutions. They began to read in national newspapers about their fellow citizens and hear the pronouncements of a national government on the radio. There was also a homogenizing of religious practice under the

[3] See Mai Yamani, 'Saudi Arabia and Central Asia: The Islamic Connection', in Anoushiravan Ehteshami (ed.), *From the Gulf to Central Asia: Players in the New Great Game* (Exeter: University of Exeter Press, 1994).
[4] Slavery was abolished by King Faisal in 1965.

dominant *hanbali* school of jurisprudence as prescribed by the established religious elite. The father's broader allegiances became synonymous with the Saudi state and beyond that with the wider causes of Arab nationalism which he would have heard articulated in Jamal Abdul Nasser's speeches on the radio. Social and geographical mobility was widespread by comparison with the previous generation. Oil money resulted in major shifts and changes in people's socio-economic status. Some became impoverished in relation to others who became very rich. Likewise, people moved from one region to another for the first time. Hence, a Hijazi might go to live in Riyadh, in the heart of Nejd, or to the Ahsa to work in the oil industry.

If the father of the family went on to higher education he probably did so at a university in the United States, where he was supported by government grants. When he returned to the Kingdom he worked in the government sector, where he was guaranteed a job. The rapid growth in government bureaucracy during the 1950s meant these newly educated workers could easily be absorbed, with the government becoming the largest employer. In the 1930s there were only two ministers, the Minister of Foreign Affairs and the Minister of Finance. During the 1950s the governing structure at the pinnacle of the Saudi state was partly institutionalized with a cabinet of over twenty ministers. During the 1970s, the wages paid by state employment in the administration or the petroleum industry allowed a man to provide for his wife, children and other dependants in the extended family – a standard of living far in excess of anything that the average member of his parents' generation could have imagined. The rapid growth of the economy owing to oil production also caused an increased demand for skilled foreign workers, who began to enter the country in large numbers for the first time since the discovery of oil. The oil economy led to large sections of the Saudi population coming into contact with Westerners and non-Muslims for the first time, as well as with other Arabs from Egypt, Palestine, Jordan, Syria and Iraq. The latter had political influence as advisers to the king and social and educational influence as teachers in schools. During the 1950s, many of these Arabs from neighbouring countries acquired Saudi citizenship. However, this trend was drastically curtailed in the 1960s, when citizenship became nearly impossible to acquire, given an attempt by the government to confine the definition of 'Saudi' to the indigenous population. This was not only a form of nationalism but also a technique of social exclusion directed at other Arabs and Muslims.

During the father's time, the state represented power and grandeur. This marked a transformation in the nature of political authority. The state acquired legitimacy and loyalty through the distribution of wealth. The response was no longer political submission but gratitude towards the generous and wealthy political patrons. Authority began to rest on the just distribution of Allah's wealth.[5]

The 'mother', although educated at one of the new schools for women, nonetheless maintained the traditional role of a woman of her generation by rearing children. However, she had the advantage of modern medicine and health care, and could make use of foreign nannies, spacious homes and modern comforts. This led to a reduction in levels of infant mortality and a baby boom that greatly increased the size of the population.

The result of that population increase is the third generation, the main focus of this book. The members of this new generation were born during the peak of the oil boom of the 1970s (1973–9) or at least before the downturn of 1984. They do not remember anything prior to oil; all notions of 'tradition', of a Bedouin past, indeed of a life lived primarily in the desert have been handed down to them through the stories and recollections of the two previous generations.

During their upbringing the members of this new generation took for granted mass education, regular travel abroad, radio and television, including, more recently, satellite broadcasts. Foreign 'servants' were a key part of their life, including nannies who assisted in bringing them up. They have been left to grapple with a very uncertain set of beliefs about 'modernity'. They know much more than their parents' generation because of their exposure to wider influences and education, but this knowledge creates problems. They have more opportunities than previous generations, but they also have more fears. They are still expected to follow their parents' 'traditions' and to listen to their instructions, but exposure to the wider world poses an increasing challenge to their fathers' authority. Change has been so swift that they still do not have the cultural terms of reference to put this new society and their role within it into perspective. The dress they wear and the food they eat represents the

---

[5] In Islam, all wealth belongs to God, and the individual is but an agent entrusted with its distribution.

complexity and tension of this situation. Western fashions inspired by satellite television and the US-dominated global culture compete with Saudi culture and national dress. The music available to them through various channels is officially banned by the *'ulama*. The youth have even encountered war in 1990–91, which added to their uneasy sense of identity. The unanswered questions that trouble the new generation are many: will they be given the chance to apply usefully the new skills and concepts learned in a greatly expanded and generously funded education system? Will they even have the guaranteed employment and the same living standards as their parents? And, crucially, who are they – what is the basis and location of their identity?

Following this amazing cultural transformation, young people lack the certainties of their grandparents, the villagers whose position and role in life appeared stable and predictable. They also lack the economic security of their parents, who grew up in a time when oil delivered plenty. The conflicting choices and uncertain future that face the new generation are seen as threatening. There are still numerous benefits (houses, food and other material goods); however, rapid urbanization has created a sense of dislocation. The move, in the space of two generations, from a self-supporting village, weakly connected to the outside world, to the cities of a modern state at the heart of a region undergoing the effects of globalization has assaulted the identity of these young people, leaving them ambivalent and troubled by an apparently superficial way of life.

The uncertainty that modernity brings can be challenged and placed in perspective by confronting its effects and questioning the outcomes. These young people, however, have not been given the personal autonomy to question a profoundly disorientating experience because of basic beliefs, traditions and religious customs that constrain and censor their thoughts and actions. One can identify two broad categories of problems with which they are grappling: first, and most noticeably, the economic transformations; and, secondly, the increasing questioning of their cultural values and norms, which are criticized as anachronistic.

Nation, family, religion and belonging: notions of tradition among the new generation

The sense of identity of the young people of Saudi Arabia described here has been taken primarily from their own thoughts and comments as expressed in their own words. In this and subsequent chapters I shall seek to explain the building blocks of the new generation's identity as derived from in-depth interviews.[6] Identity is key to any individual, allowing one to place oneself within the family, community and wider society. An individual's identity has many strands, each assuming different importance depending on the situation. These strands or forms of identity range from the most pervasive – the family – to the tribe, the region and, more recently, the city. Despite state-driven attempts to foster Saudi national identity and even to develop a 'Gulf' identity, Saudi Arabia, though united in a single national unit in 1932, remains a heterogeneous country. National and wider 'Gulf' identity must compete with and often comes second to the family and the four regions as prime units of allegiance.

Those interviewed attach a high significance to the persistence of institutions that are familiar to their parents and grandparents and that remain important to the new generation's self-conceptions. Tradition is seen by the new generation in terms of religion and culture. Young people deploy these values alongside the sense of belonging to the state and the wider Arab community. The use of the term 'nation' is problematical in this regard: although portrayed by the institutions of the state as traditional and unchanging, it is for many a novelty with ambiguous connotations. However, this ambiguity the youth sometimes express has not prevented the emergence of a strong sense of national belonging. A shared sense of cultural difference from both Westerners and others in the wider Arab world has fostered a cultural commonality at both the national and wider Gulf levels that overshadows regional or tribal distinctions.

Tradition is represented through vivid images, usually drawn from family life. For example, when I asked Saad (16), from the Hijaz, to describe aspects of tradition he said, 'Tradition is family reunion,' and 'It is when the *zabiha* (the whole lamb) is presented to eat.' Asma (28), from

---

[6] The age, home town and social category of the young men and women interviewed is provided in the appendix.

Jeddah, defines tradition as 'the things people always do as their parents and grandparents did'. Said (27), from Tabuk, said that tradition was following the prophet Mohammad's practices through his authenticated *hadith* (sayings). Linking tradition to their parents' way of life not only means obedience to family and religion but seems to lessen fears about change and uncertainty. The new generation appears to have created a sense of being rooted in what it sees as the traditional institution of the family, which provides a link to the continuity of the past. At times of serious change in their way of life, young people's link with 'tradition' gives them a sense of security and a sense of identity. Adnan (24), from Mecca, said that 'tradition is respect shown towards older people'. Malak (17), from Jeddah, says that she admires the *ihtiram* (respect) of tradition. However, she worries that the respect paid to the past is rapidly diminishing. She says that it used to be important to be *bint an-nas* ('the daughter of good people') and to follow tradition, but now people do not necessarily admire self-respect and good lineage. Concerned about the pace of change, she agrees that 'in order to be part of the global village, we need to become more international'. But she hastily adds that 'we must keep something for ourselves'. In other words, she thinks that local identity has to be maintained to give coherence to both the individual and society in the midst of changing circumstances.

Hamad (29), from a southern tribe in Asir, voices a more critical opinion about tradition: 'The older generation generally does not allow the younger to take over, basically because fathers are very jealous of their sons.' But Hamad qualifies and dilutes this assertion by saying that he likes tradition, especially some 'beautiful traditional rules such as the respect for elders and other customs that prevent calamities and provide security'. But there are for Hamad some traditions which should be swept away; for example, if a man dies his brother should not have to marry his widow. Despite this, 'marrying one's first cousin is a good thing, as long as the woman is not obliged to marry against her will'.

Said wants to emulate the values of his parents' generation. 'I want to be just like my father. I admire his wisdom, his reactions and the way he handles problems. There is so much to learn from the older generation.' This is despite the fact that Said's father is illiterate, 'but he has always had an instinctive ability with numbers, making him a good business-man'.

Nouf (23), a member of the royal family, exemplifies the conflict of perceptions experienced by most members of the new generation. She says that she values Islam, especially the *salafi* approach, a *wahhabi* concept calling for the purification of Islam and the return to basic Islamic principles. She sees this approach as linked to the purity of desert architecture and the strength of the Arabic language. Socially she thinks it is religiously incumbent upon Saudi youth to maintain the existence of the extended family as well as the traditional segregation of the sexes because generally conservative Islamic trends 'preserve society'. Yet she holds these views in conjunction with a perception of herself as a 'liberal'. She sees herself as open to positive change derived from the wider world and as having the ability to adapt to changing circumstances. Crucially, however, for Nouf this must go hand in hand with holding on to a deeper sense of identity related to her parents' generation. Without this continuity and stability she believes her peers would get lost in a confusing and morally ambiguous world.

This illustration shows that for many the source for rules of social conduct and for religious observance are one and the same. Indeed, people are often at pains to demonstrate that their particular traditions have roots in or are at least sanctioned by a reading of religious texts and sayings. For others religion has acquired a wider significance, above and beyond the family. Community, for these people, is frequently defined in religious terms. Faiz (16), like many others who have travelled and been exposed to the Western world, sees Islam as the focus of his identity. He states: 'All tradition is important, religion is tradition.'

The symbolism of Islam combined with the unique heritage of Saudi Arabia based on the guardianship of Mecca and Medina continue to be central to the Saudi identity and therefore to many Saudis' sense of political and social stability. Adnan is typical of many who link tradition and their sense of belonging to religion. When asked about his family background, he says that they were *'ulama* who taught at the Great Mosque in Mecca. 'I wish that I were living in the days of my grand-fathers to learn from them.' When asked where his values and morality come from he refers to them being specifically Muslim values. Nouf is more specific in her definition of tradition and religion. It is *'salafi* and pure desert Nejdi culture'. She criticizes Sufi practices because 'they efface the individual, which *salafi* Islam celebrates'.

The members of the new generation appreciate that their traditions relate to what they and their families and neighbours used to do, not what others did. Jamila, Asia, Amel and Ahlam (cousins between eighteen and twenty-one, from Jeddah) define tradition as norms that were transmitted from one generation to another; some of the norms stem from religion but most are social. 'The new generation knows how to question and should have the freedom to choose its tradition,' Amel says, adding that each family has its own culture and that what one family thinks is right may not apply to another family in the same community.

More pertinent and serious is the new generation's questioning of the consistency and cohesion of the traditions of the ruling elite. Haifa (16) strongly defends morality and local traditions. She believes that traditions in the Hijaz, especially with regard to women's status, are different from those in Nejd. The Hijaz has always been advanced, but Riyadh (the capital in Nejd) has developed fast and is catching up, although regional distinctiveness still exists. Traditions for Haifa and Nouf, as for others, are relative – specific to a generation, to a region or to a religious expression. In response to a question on whether the segregation of the sexes in educational and professional spheres should be maintained, Adnan described the practice as 'backward, the origins of which had nothing to do with religion, but were more associated with the cultural practices of the Bedouin'. He cited *ayyam al-sahaba* (days of the prophet's companions) as proof that gender segregation did not exist. Jamila, Asia, Amel and Ahlam also think the government has its own opinion on tradition. 'Nowadays what tradition says is wrong the government says is *sah* (correct) because they are trying to gain the *rida* (contentment of the people). For example, banks that are based on *riba* (interest) are forbidden by the *mashaikh* (religious authorities); however, the government is dealing with these banks.'

The new generation tries to relate the various and sometimes competing communities to which it feels it belongs. Although family is the most important unit of identity it is accompanied by an increasing sense of national belonging. Religion is often given greater prominence than both nation and family because it allows for other competing allegiances to be subsumed into the larger category. Sultan (15) believes that national identity is most important. Omar (16) agrees; he opposes tribalism, saying it is divisive: 'All Saudi Arabians should unite.' Ahmed (21) attaches importance to the nation first and family second; he does not mention the region. But Saad (16) contradicts this, saying, 'I am first a Hijazi.' He believes that regional identity has the longest history and is the strongest. Rasha (27) also considers herself a Hijazi. For Samir (15) the regional Gulf identity is important: 'The tribe today has no meaning, except for those living in the villages. Gulf values were born in a plot of land; we have the basis for cooperation, but we need changes in education in Gulf countries in order to reach this objective.' However, there is an ambiguity in the general appeal of 'tradition' among the new generation. The Saudi state since 1932 has not only used a notion of 'tradition' to legitimate itself, but through actively sponsoring cultural, religious and political unification has also created a new, distinctly national notion of tradition. When questioned during group interviews about the importance of values, many of the respondents attached importance to Islamic identity first and then a national identity. Many in the new generation see religion as the primary defining factor of their lives, giving them a moral purpose. Abdul Karim (23) expressed this by calling himself first a Muslim and secondly a Saudi and an Arab. He attaches importance to nation and family, declaring that 'all Saudis are brothers'. Jassem (23) defines tradition as compatibility with religion. He too believes that Saudi traditions are important, especially the extended family and the segregation of the sexes in public spheres. Jassem also attaches importance to nation and family. He identifies himself as a Muslim first and then as a Saudi and Arab. He says: 'The Lebanese or the Egyptians are not my brothers. Today in our country we deal with people through Islam.' Likewise, Arif (27) and Mansour (30) say their sense of identity is first as a Muslim, then as a Saudi and Arab. Mansour also attaches importance to nation and family. According to Salman (25), 'Of the different levels of identity, being a Muslim is most important to me, followed by being a Saudi and coming from the GCC area. As for levels of belonging, the family is most important, followed by the nation and then lastly the region from which I come.'

Exposure to modernity

There is widespread participation among the new generation in social practices that have been introduced since their parents' day or that have become more available. People have far greater access to print and electronic media, including satellite as well as domestic television, the Internet and a variety of publications. Participation, however, is far from uniform. There are differences related to wealth, education and language acquisition. For the new generation the idea of progress is associated with the need to absorb modern technologies into practical life. Some social relations are associated with modernity: the democratization of family life, for instance, and other matters relating to gender can often be seen in terms of Western social values. The young people interviewed have two main ways of encountering the wider world – the media, including the Internet, and foreign travel. Restrictions on access to the media within Saudi Arabia are a persistent source of controversy.

Access to the media is ubiquitous among those interviewed. There are some expected differences between them all based on language, interests, and exposure to other countries. Jamila, Asia, Amel and Ahlam do not speak English. Nevertheless they watch a wide range of channels, and do so for different reasons. Jamila loves news – Orbit news, CNN, periodicals – and she can now understand *Iqtisadiyya* (similar to *The Economist*). She also loves MTV and America Plus (a series about high school girls and boys). Amel prefers radio to TV; she likes news on the Arab satellite MBC and FM. She likes MBC and Arabic channels. Ahlam reads *Okaz* and *Iqtisadiyya* but she thinks that contact with people offers more than the media. Manal (17) watches television and prefers Western films 'because Arabic movies are very badly produced'. She reads *Al-Sharq-Al-Awsat* newspaper and Arabic magazines such as *Sayyidati*, but also the *Independent*, which her family can access in Jeddah. Manal reads both Arabic and English but prefers Arabic 'because it is closer to us and the realities of our societies. England is an alien society.'

For many of these young people, the primary value of access to the media is the entertainment value. For example, Hind (19) and her sister read local society magazines, watch MBC and Egyptian television. They do not read any books outside their school curriculum and have very little knowledge of international events. Yassir (22) watches television, especially the US comedy 'Seinfeld'. He also likes Orbit television, although there is no demand for certain programmes that are beneficial, such as Discovery: 'People are just not interested.' Yassir is interested in magazines for cars, especially those for specialists. 'Unfortunately, Arabic magazines of that sort are no good because the technical words are lost.' Yassir approves of the magazine *Arrajul:* 'Although it is very expensive, costing 35 riyals, you can see that the producers worked hard on it.' Yassir listens to MBC, and FM radio in order to keep up to date with Arabic songs, and to some of the Arabic programmes: 'The minute we get into a car, if the cassette is not available, MBC is on.' Abdul Hamid (23), who watches television and prefers movie channels, uses the Internet while in England because it is not available for the public in Saudi Arabia. Abdul Karim says that local television presents discussions about issues without giving solutions. 'Everything is so complicated because of censorship, so people end up watching wrestling.'

Other young people place a higher value on the media for the access it gives them to information and the help it provides for their education. Haifa (16) believes that television is the most important source of information. 'We know all that happens from television.' She hardly reads any books, although she reads some Arabic magazines. Mansour travels between Saudi Arabia and London, but he has also been to the United States, Europe, other GCC countries and Egypt. He watches television, especially programmes that deal with the mind, such as BBC shows and *Imad Al-Din* talk shows on Orbit. Mansour reads *Al-Hayat, Al-Sharq-Al-Awsat,* the *International Herald Tribune* and *Time* magazine. He uses the Internet and believes it is generally very beneficial. Mansour believes that technology is important and rates the different sources of information in order: television first, then newspapers, magazines and radio.

Amina (18) reads *Al-Sharq-Al-Awsat* and watches MBC television, as do all her friends, and listens to *Saut Al-Arab* from Monte Carlo: 'Technology, such as computers, is absolutely crucial, but the most important thing for a career and one's own education is literacy.' Malak says: 'I watch films and MTV on satellite. I like pop music. Technology is very important. It connects Saudi Arabia to the whole world. The Internet is very limited in Saudi Arabia; a lot is censored.'

The issue of censorship is perplexing for Hamad (29), whose favourite television channel is Al Jazira, a political satellite broadcast from

Qatar. He considers that Al Jazira fills a gap and makes people aware of political debates that concern them. 'Four years ago we did not know about oil problems, or two years ago about the stock exchange crisis. People now receive this information from Al Jazira.' Interestingly, he has a low opinion of Western satellite television. It 'has negative effects on the youth, because many blindly imitate what they see, from clothes and appearances to dancing to a song that you don't even understand the words to. People have lost their identity. It is as if a spell has been put on them, transforming them into distorted figures.'

Travelling abroad is an option available to many of the new generation. In many ways, travel has an impact on their views and opinions, especially when they can speak English. However, closer contact with other cultures often reinforces a sense of belonging to one's own community. The results of extensive travel are illustrated by Said (27), who says that since his graduation he has been travelling 'a lot'. He has been to Britain and plans to go to the United States. Yet he cannot communicate in English despite his three months in London and his degree in business administration. Amina, from Jeddah, said her education for one year in England taught her how to depend on herself and not to be entirely dependent on the family. 'But you also learn compassion for Muslims. In Saudi Arabia I learnt about religion. I couldn't have learnt it anywhere else.'

There is no doubt about the considerable enthusiasm among many in the new generation for what modernity has to offer. Twenty-four-year-old Adnan's feelings about travelling to the United States encapsulate this more expansive view. He values it because he 'can find anything there', as well as enjoying the beaches and entertainment. Mish'al (29), from Riyadh, says he gained a lot of his positive attributes from his exposure to the culture of the United States. His experience abroad opened his mind. It made him realize that 'there is freedom of expression both in professional and personal contexts' and that 'you can make anything of yourself because in the West everything is possible'. He watches satellite television, especially CNN or educational programmes. He says that he would never watch the local Saudi media. 'If I were fifteen I would look down on what I study because what I see on the satellite shows that everything or anything is possible.' Saad (16) likes to travel to countries in the Arab world because 'when I go to Western countries Saudi Arabia is always on my mind'. However, he likes Dubai because 'you can get a taste of what you are missing in Saudi Arabia but still feel at home'. Saad is constantly using the Internet. He mostly likes television programmes that have music. He thinks that 'technology in Saudi Arabia will contribute to breaking down barriers, especially the Internet as it becomes cheaper to be exposed to different people'.

There is a deep and widespread unease that modernity may well entail more than just the acquisition of technology. For many, modernity brings Western values that threaten Saudi traditions. Saad, for instance, thinks that tradition is not a static concept but must change with social developments. He defines modernity as changing the old for the new. 'Sometimes there is a clash between tradition and modernity. In Saudi Arabia there is a lot more modernity than tradition. We must improve our traditions by choosing the valuable ones, such as family gatherings at meal times, but progress is healthy.' Ghalib (17) recognizes that modernity is driven by technological advancement but says that it should not be at the expense of tradition. Adnan defines modernity more cautiously, both technologically and socially: 'Modernity is to respect the past and to build the future on it.'

Despite this enthusiasm for the goods and opportunities made available through the development of increased market access to the West, there is a general apprehension of possible contradictions between what the new generation values as traditional and modern cultures. Some young people gave accounts of their personal experiences of struggle over the introduction of new practices and social innovations, largely located within the family and political arenas.

The home is the site of greatest impact of the new electronic media technologies. There are evident tensions between the modern and the traditional which affect life within the home. This can be the case regardless of wealth or status. Nouf finds that she is still searching for a balance between being a Saudi princess and all the 'rebellious ideas' she is exposed to in the West. At the moment, she describes herself as rebellious but says her immediate family is understanding. Said, on the other hand, comes from a rural village where his parents are illiterate. Sources of cultural exposure were extremely limited, with the radio providing the main window on the outside world until 1977, when television arrived. New forms of media were not welcomed by his mother, who used her 'strength and dominance in the family' to oppose the latest intrusion, a satellite dish. Said explains that this is because she cared about her sons and daughters and wanted to protect them from 'the dangers of Western corruption'. But after several years the family convinced her, and Said has had access to satellite television since 1993. In the span of sixteen years Said has witnessed the widening and ultimate transformation of his cultural sphere and has had immediate experience of the personal conflicts this entailed.

At a time of major changes in the social structure, the question of tradition and modernity obviously preoccupies the youth, whatever their socio-economic or regional background and irrespective of gender. Salman explains the tensions in the system realistically. 'There are tensions here between modernity and tradition. There was tension with the *'ulama* when radio was successfully introduced. There is still tension over women's education and satellite dishes but the wheels of evolution will not stop, cannot stop turning.'

There are deeply conflicting pressures from contemporary political and economic forces. The state and religious authorities show great reluctance to permit general access to some forms of modern communication. Yassir, when asked about the Internet, replied jokingly, 'What is the Internet?', referring to the official reluctance to introduce it in Saudi Arabia. However, he acknowledged that the Internet and satellite television were 'a double-edged weapon'. But when asked whether Saudi society should open up more, he said it had already opened up to the outside world.

Despite state-sponsored efforts to restrict what can be watched on domestic television, there is nonetheless a greater variety available on satellite television, both Western and Arab channels. The state-run media have lost their dominance over young people. The drab presentation and limited scope of issues covered on Saudi television mean that it has increasingly been rejected, and attention has also been drawn to the issue of censorship. Sami (30), from Jeddah, was critical of local censorship, claiming that Saudi television was commonly referred to as *'ghasb* (force-feeding) Channel 1 and *ghasb* Channel 2'. As for media exposure: 'If I have the Internet, I will ignore all other sources of information. But we will never get the Internet because we are dependent; we have a lot of censorship in Saudi. I would never read a Saudi newspaper because it has nothing of substance in it.'

Abdul Aziz (30), who is representative of the more 'conservative' perception of modernity and tradition, was also critical of Saudi television: 'There is nothing in the channels that benefits the *umma*, Islamic nation; both Channels 1 and 2 specialize in "shoving things down our throats".' But, interestingly, Abdul Aziz is also critical about satellite television: 'It has a dangerous influence, especially channels like Al Jazira.' More generally, he thinks that the disadvantages of satellite television outweigh its advantages: 'It has a negative influence on our traditions and customs, also negatively affecting the morality of the young generation, especially such channels as MTV. In fact, the main aim of these channels is to influence our values.' Abdul Aziz refers to the 'Jewish–Western conspiracy'. He is convinced that those who 'control' satellite broadcasting have an agenda negatively to influence the younger generation in Saudi Arabia. Meanwhile, the Saudi government, by emphasizing such things as football, has not exposed this danger to the nation. The youth have not been encouraged to 'put their thinking caps on'. Sahar (30), from Jeddah, is a liberal and shares the feeling that state-run media services are restrictive and have a negative influence. She says: 'Censorship is hated by everybody. It has nothing to do with our values.' She thinks that freedom of expression is related to progress.

The ambivalence among most young people is captured by Mish'al, who comments: 'I like tradition. I like to sit like this and eat with my hands. Why should I pick up my cup of tea in an English fashion? It has no history in my country.' But he goes on to comment: 'For Saudi Arabia to become part of the global society, it needs to open its borders, and strict social rules should be abolished. People must be given more opportunities.'

The real threat to the lives and experiences of members of communities in Saudi Arabia posed by the new technologies is nonetheless taken quite seriously by most of the young. There is no blanket acceptance of new technologies, even by those who have unrestricted access to them. Hadi (23), from Riyadh, uses the Internet but believes that access should be selective. 'For example, it should not access things that contradict the Islamic religion.' Ahmed watches a lot of television but he believes that satellite television is both very destructive and very informative. It is destructive because it encourages ideas that are unsuitable for 'our environment', such as those presented on the 'Jerry Springer' programme.

Direct contact with Westerners or things perceived to be Western can also raise difficult questions. When Ayman (16) was asked whether travelling to Europe and the United States had a significant impact on his values, he said that it had advantages and disadvantages. 'It is good to learn English to get away from one's own world and to forget problems as well as to relax, but the disadvantage could be losing Islamic values.' Ayman believes that 'even when abroad a person must preserve his identity by being in touch with the country and heritage'. That said, members of the new generation think that maintaining Saudi identity is difficult when contact with the West is needed in order to advance.

There is a wide recognition that modernity involves being judged according to alien standards as cultures increasingly share, even compete for, the same physical spaces. Precisely which standards should be applied to others or which are being applied to one's own conduct is a problem. For Manal this is a matter of being subject to greater restrictions in Saudi Arabia than when abroad. She says that her father takes things easy in England, 'but when we arrive in Saudi Arabia, we have to hear "do this, like this, or else what will people say?"'. Maha (17) finds this a problem and thinks that modernity clashes with the traditional in Saudi Arabia. Malak also sees modernity as having a negative effect: 'Young people have the wrong attitude, a selfish attitude to modernism.'

For conservatives, modern social practices appear to be incompatible with virtues. The very term 'open-minded' seems to capture a sense of profligacy of personality, persons without restraint or practical control over themselves and their relations with the world. A large number of those interviewed are aware of the tensions but they do not regard modern goods as bad in themselves. There is a widespread feeling that these goods and practices can be put to good use, provided they are approached in the right spirit. For some, especially among those who have had the greatest exposure to the West, having been educated in English and having adopted liberal terminology as well as practical goods, the direction of tensions is reversed. For liberals, the need to survive and achieve in the contemporary world requires a more open-minded attitude.

These general attitudes can be investigated in relation to the issues of indirect contact between groups through technology and the media, of direct contact between groups via travel, tourism and immigration, and of attitudes towards relations between generations. The comments of the new generation are increasingly expressing a more individualistic morality of personal achievement while recognizing and lamenting a falling off of social solidarity. The market, as opposed to the family or community, takes on greater significance and the terms in which evaluations are made are increasingly oriented towards that market mentality, rather than the community.

Conclusion

Over the past few years, pre-existing economic, political and religious behavioural standards have come under increasing pressure within Saudi Arabia. This has resulted in old standards of behaviour being either discarded or modified, a process that has inevitably resulted in the reinvention of new levels and forms of identity. This has generated an ambiguity of outlook, embracing technology and the information it brings while seeking security in a modification and reinvention of the tradition that permeates the identity of the new generation. For some, their perception of tradition allows them to interact with a changing and possibly threatening world from a position of certainty. The shift towards market-oriented practices has had a considerable effect on attitudes towards what the young conceive of as older institutions. The heightened awareness of the family as a unit of reference can be related to this. Families are no longer the dominant sphere of socio-economic life; their role appears to be becoming gradually marginalized. Valorizing the family is a recognition of its diminished role in life. Something similar can be said of religion. There is a shift in the relationship between religion and the more market-based social life. Religion either adjusts to this by becoming less concrete and more permissive, or adopts a more rigorous enforcement of certain concrete social practices.

Those who take tradition and community seriously argue that the state and family should see to it that the tensions between the old and the new are minimized. To this end, they argue for measures to reinforce a sense of national community. Respect for tradition and the older generation means that people should not be exposed to things that will 'shock their minds'. Osama (16), from Riyadh, believes that it is good for Saudi society to remain isolated. 'It is a form of protection because laws will change; customs, food, the whole society will change too fast. The values of our parents' generation were based on seriousness. For our generation everything is available.' Amina (18) enjoyed her travels and Western exposure but does not believe that too much questioning is good. 'In Saudi Arabia you can learn how to control your behaviour and to respect. Most of the time you cannot say what you think, which is good.'

Yet others see no alternative to some form of convergence between themselves and the West. Adnan did not accept that social distance should be maintained between foreigners and Saudis. When asked with which categories of expatriates he thought Saudis ought to have closer contact, he responded that 'this decision should not be based on nationality but rather on profession'. Asked whether he thought Saudi Arabia was isolated and needed to open up to the outside world, he answered affirmatively. Ahmed's view of relations with the expatriates is that 'we should learn from their experiences and absorb what is beneficial from their cultures'.

On the one hand, as mentioned above, there is a tendency towards the marginalization of the significance of the family as a socio-economic force. Saad believes that in Saudi Arabia there is much more modernity than tradition. Saad sees that tradition is not a static concept and must change with social developments, even if this means reducing the significance of family just to occasional gatherings.

On the other hand, there is the marginalization and diminution of the significance of religion. Ayman believes that there is no future for those who study *shari'a* at university and that the development of a more secular national identity is important. Naif believes that 'all we should maintain from tradition is the Islamic theological nucleus, and that's all'. He objects to traditions such as the segregation of the sexes. As for modernity, the main debate revolves around what is Islamic versus non-Islamic: 'In this debate I am not sure where I stand. I am non-Islamic here.'

Religion can be changed by shifting its concerns towards the secular world and finding ways of adapting it to that world. An increase in the use of a 'social' language dealing with matters of economic and social justice might be expected to accompany these kinds of developments. For example, Abdullah (26), from Najran, does not believe that there are problems with introducing the Internet into Saudi Arabia because there is flexibility in Islam. He used the term 'Islamic infiltration' in his attempt to explain that we can adapt technology to belief. 'Our religion is for all, without distinction between poor or rich until we die. What is happening today is that access to technology is open to some and not to others.'

Identity is always a social and a collective matter. Erik Erikson's theory of identity formation stresses that:

[a] sense of identity means a sense of being at one with oneself as one grows and develops; and it means, at the same time, a sense of affinity with a community's sense of being at one with its future as well as its history – or mythology. ... Individuals only feel at home in the world if they develop a strong sense of personal, individual identity which resonates with and finds its validity in an accompanying collective identity. Individual identities only can be formed within stable group identities: the term expresses ... a mutual relation in that it connotes both a persistent sameness within oneself (selfsameness) and a persistent sharing of some kind of essential character with others.[7]

Identity, whether conceptualized as 'given' (natural) or 'constructed' (social) is that which endows groups and individuals with a place, a function, a purpose and, in the modern world, with the capacity for action.[8] So identity is indivisible from modern politics. The basis of an individual's identity within a given society is over-determined, being created from numerous sources. Each input gains or loses importance depending on the individual's social circumstances the individual is in. Since the founding of the state, Saudi identity has been determined by overlapping and competing sources. Internal sources of competition have included religion, tribal belonging, family and the nation. External sources have encompassed the forces of Western modernization. The direction of this evolving sense of identity has been linked to the processes of economic development and government policy. The ruling elite has sought to control the process in ways that support its own political agenda and strengthen its position at the heart of the state. In times of economic growth, the Saudi population, optimistic about the future and supported by a financially strong state, has received ideas from the

[7] Kathryn Dean, 'Introduction', in Kathryn Dean (ed.), *Politics and the Ends of Identity* (Aldershot, Hants: Ashgate, 1997).
[8] Ibid.

outside world with a degree of confidence that facilitates their coherent assimilation. However, in times of economic uncertainty and government austerity (the current Saudi context), the population as a whole tends to seek cultural reassurance in notions of tradition. They become pre-occupied with the mosque and public displays of piety or the home village from which their grandparents came, or else they transfigure the meaning of tradition so that it fits more easily with the new world. Either way, this retreat into certainty is an attempt to interact with a rapidly changing and uncertain world from a secure and recognizable base.

Erik Erikson suggests that there is a need to relate the various aspects of one's life to one another in a relatively coherent way. That modern institutions, practices and goods have changed life for many, and in significant ways, is beyond dispute. The problem of rapid change in the institutional frameworks of the lives of succeeding generations is that it gives rise to inter-generational conflicts in interpreting the character of both the old and the new. Reconciling these differences, or finding ways of living with them, is the stuff of life for the new generation.

2 National identity and political aspirations

The third generation, today's youth, represents the full embodiment of the national identity that originated with the establishment of the state of Saudi Arabia in 1932. Regional or tribal identities have been tamed, giving prominence to a more pronounced sense of national identity. Relations between members of the small, locally based communities of the grandparents' generation were regulated by moral codes that imposed duties and responsibilities on all members, and, of course, the moral language of the community drew heavily on Islam. The last two generations have seen the emergence of far broader senses of community that have developed at the national level. For many, the older communities have been replaced, or at least added to, by the nation. Despite the change in the size and nature of the community, and despite the less personal relations between people of different status, the language in which people express their sense of national belonging still draws heavily on the language of 'tradition' and Islam.

The previous chapter explored the new generation's sense of social identity and its ambiguous position between tradition and modernity. While the theme of identity was introduced with discussion of its different forms and levels, the familial, tribal and religious, the aim of the work is to examine each component of identity separately. This chapter focuses on the national identity that has been established and the experiences and perceptions of the new generation's 'Saudiness'.

The comments of this generation show that there has been a significant change in the use of moral language. Many of the comments expressed would have been inconceivable in the 1970s, when attitudes towards authority were more subservient and relations between the ruled and rulers, between 'inferiors' and 'superiors' better defined. Young people's vision of the world and the way in which the nation, the region, the tribe and the international system relate to one another has been transformed. While their parents identified the future with the possibilities for positive change, the members of the new generation seem to think that change means uncertainty and doubt. By and large, they fear further change, thinking that things will only get worse. Consequently this generation is much more prepared to express its dissatisfaction with what it sees as the double standards of those who have authority within society. High status, which should be worthy of respect, is increasingly seen as a means to gain immunity from the moral strictures of society and the laws of the state. This new generation expresses a demand for a more equitable system, not one based on tribal hierarchy or social distinctions derived from birth into an elite family, as well as a desire for fairness and for the young to be taken more seriously as key members of the national political community. Young people in today's Saudi Arabia are calling for greater freedom of expression, criticizing censorship. They feel that the state's concern for secrecy is in reality a screen for moral and economic failings, a means of concealing and evading the truth. Most single out the *mutaw'a* and religious authorities for criticism, claiming they impose too many constraints. The youth, however, are not saying that they do not want moral rules but rather are demanding that the law be based on a more flexible interpretation of Islam. Their Islam is less confined. Islam continues to be, for them, the basis of legitimate behaviour, but the way it is enforced by the authorities is seen as too restrictive. Most young people whose views were solicited for this study do believe that it is the state's role to enforce and guard religion and that those in authority should uphold the highest moral values in their own public and private lives. Indeed, the ruling family, the Al-Saud, are identified as the protectors of Islam, but they do not tend to be regarded as executing or enforcing this authority correctly.

This current generation takes for granted both the national community and the state as a key part of its world. However, relations between these two features of modern Saudi life, the community on the one hand and the state on the other, are not straightforward. From the standpoint of the Islamic national community the political, legal and bureaucratic institutions of the state are widely held in rather low regard: they face persistent questions about their moral status. Generally speaking, they are considered to be spheres in which moral conduct is often poor and people fall short of their duties to the community and to Islam.

There are two principal perceptions of the causes of these problems. For some, the relationship of the elites of the Kingdom with external Western powers, especially the United States, is seen to be the main problem. By relying on foreign support for its power, state authority has lost touch with domestic concerns. For others, there remains the problem of tribal fissures within the national community. Those who exercise political authority are seen as doing so not in the interests of the nation as a whole but rather in a narrow and excluding way. In either case, the attempts to claim moral authority on the grounds of adherence to Islamic values are seen to ring somewhat hollow.

The solutions suggested to this problem of legitimacy, however, depend mainly on the development of a sense of communal responsibility guided by Islamic tenets. Of course, this covers a very wide range of possible ideas about behavioural or institutional change. However, there are also other voices, which in a local Islamic context appear more extreme: that of the radical *salafis*[1] and another that uses language drawn from the secular West. Political democratization and economic liberalization are seen by the second group as the best way of limiting political power and ensuring its moral quality.

Some of the most significant political reforms to have taken place in Saudi Arabia in recent times occurred between 1992 and 1993. In March 1992 the king issued the Basic Law and two texts defining the characteristics of a consultative council and the role of the regions. In September of the same year, 107 prominent men addressed a 45-page memorandum to the late Shaykh 'Abd Al-Aziz bin Baz, the highest religious official in the country at that time. This document articulated widely held concerns. It did not question the role and status of the King. Instead, it called for political authority to be established on the basis of a number of principles: equality before the law; official accountability; elimination of corruption and usury; redistribution of wealth; reinforcement of the army and national independence; and restricted powers for the police. In August 1993, the king appointed a 60-member *majlis al-shura* (consultative council), for the most part selecting members of 'modern elites', with only nominal representation of the *'ulama*. These events highlighted the changing structure of national political life in Saudi Arabia and

[1] *Salafi* is a wahhabi concept calling for the purification of Islam and the return to the basic original Islamic principles.

demonstrated people's desire for change. Most significantly, they drew attention to the emergence of 'modern elites', to the entry of the new middle class into political life. Before moving on to explore young people's views, the following section will consider the processes that have produced a shift in authority towards this new class, and the popular attitudes that have accompanied this movement.

Political background

National identity formation in Saudi Arabia has three main facets. The first is the consolidation of the core of the nation around the ruling family. The Al-Saud have successfully secured themselves within a substantial network of traditional relationships, based on family, lineage, tribe, region and religion. The second facet is the development of the institutional framework of the state on the basis of extensive infrastructural programmes and the expansion of its bureaucratic apparatus. This was facilitated by abundant oil revenues. The state has used employment and the distribution of benefits as vehicles to draw people from beyond the core constituency of Al-Saud power into the nation. The third aspect of this process is the development of a national political culture. This is based largely on Nejdi heritage and is spoken of in terms of tradition, heavily reliant on a particular version of Islam. This culture provides the language of both legitimization and criticism of political authority. These three processes have not developed without tensions emerging among them, mainly because the growth of the state has given rise to new social groups which make demands for political and economic inclusion in the nation. Economically, reductions in the resources available to the ruling elite for distribution to these groups place strains on the patrimonial structure of the state, where the traditional social and moral practices of paternalism have been adapted to the new conditions of a modern bureaucratic system. Politically, the moral discourse of power and authority is turned against the state as people sense their continuing and deepening exclusion.

At the core of the nation is 'an oligarchy whose pillars are the Saudi royal house, the *'ulama* and the *umara'*.[2] Its success has rested in part on

---

[2] Mordechai Abir, 'The Consolidation of the Ruling Class and the New Elites in Saudi Arabia', *Middle Eastern Studies*, Vol. 23, No. 2, 1987, pp. 154–5.

its ability to hold together an alliance based on traditional ties. Government has often oriented its actions towards maintaining the cohesion of this group and therefore is conducted on the two principles of *shura* (consultation in Islamic tradition) and *ijma'* (consensus) within the ruling class.[3] As a result, the Al-Saud have successfully maintained a high degree of organic solidarity as a patronymic group while becoming the national elite. The ruling family controls all important government positions and has strengthened its base of support by alliances with the religious establishment, the Al-Shaykh, and the regional elites. The princes of Al-Saud number 6,000 and, combined with the Al-Shaykh, number as many as 12,000 men. This core of 12,000 are related by marriage to all the other local lineages, such as the Sudayris, making the ruling class around 20,000 strong. Together with other non-royal partners, the Kingdom's elite total as many 100,000. Thus, the influence and socio-economic demands of such a substantial ruling class can never be underestimated.

Within this core is an unofficial leadership known as the *ahl al-hal wal-'aqd* (those who bind and loose). Public knowledge about this authoritative and powerful body of about 100 senior figures is rather limited, although it is largely accepted that it is not institutionalized in a formal sense. It includes Al-Abd Al-Rahman Al-Saud and cadet branches of the family and draws on another fifty members of aristocratic families closely allied to the Sauds, namely the Jilwi, Sudayri, Thunayan and Al-Shaykh. There are also some prominent *'ulama* and a small number of highly consequential *umara*. 'The criteria for membership in *ahl al-hal wal-'aqd*, it seems, are origin, seniority, prestige and leadership qualities, according to Bedouin tradition.'[4]

The royal family follows a traditional pattern of rule: the distribution of patronage, both in the form of influence over public-sector jobs and by the provision of welfare schemes for the remainder of the population, remains the material basis of its rule. Other areas of state patronage have been the provision of free health care and education and subsidies for medicine, bread, electric power and petrol. The state also offers interest-free loans and gifts of land. There is the novel phenomenon of men relying on state welfare for a $5,000 gift for the marriage dower,

[3] Ibid.
[4] Ibid.

supported by the state to encourage marriages between Saudi nationals. Thus the state has attempted to maintain the patrimonial structure. The system of monarchic rule is a form of patronage, depending on the immense oil wealth controlled by the Al-Saud.

One of the most striking ways in which the state has developed has been through its employment of the overwhelming majority of the population. This pattern has given rise to the emergence of new social classes. Indeed, the new middle class first gained access to government posts of a higher rank in the 1960s as the administration expanded and more and more Saudis returned from universities abroad.[5] This new middle class developed with the spread of modern education, state employment and rapid urbanization, all of which has enabled increasing numbers to gain access to modern occupations. Without direct personal ties to the political elites, these salaried middle classes developed within the state apparatus but did so relatively autonomously from the old patronage systems. They found themselves bound together by common urban and educational experiences that separated them from the old elite. This new generation was more exposed to the growth of the 'modern' identities of profession, class and ideology.

In seeking to secure their dominance over new social classes, the ruling elites sought to develop a national political culture. As a result, national identity has been largely based on the state projection of Nejdi political and religious culture. Nejdi standards of economic, political, social and religious behaviour have been imposed on society as a whole. For example, all Saudi nationals had to drop their regional dress and adopt that of the Nejd. The homogenization of the four previously distinctive provinces into a Saudi nation has to a great extent been successful. Regional identity was amalgamated into the central dominant power. The prevailing political climate in Saudi Arabia precludes overt expressions of regional identity as separate from that of the state. Thus the consolidation of power has been accomplished through the creation of national homogeneity.

Saudi political culture is the common ground between society and the state, between rulers and ruled. As such it should be seen as a tool used by the elites to impose their will on society from above. 'When its significance

---

[5] William Rugh, 'The Emergence of a New Middle Class in Saudi Arabia', *Middle East Journal*, Vol. 27, No. 1, Winter 1973, p. 13.

in the political process is acknowledged, its role is often reduced to that of an ideology, upon which the ruling group builds its legitimacy.'[6] Rather, this political culture is best regarded as both an enabling ideology and a constraining force. A key aspect of this political culture has been religion. The ruling elites have institutionalized the religious authorities in an attempt to use Islam for their own political legitimation. Since the rise to power of Abdul Aziz Al-Saud, the *'ulama* have had to depend on the government for their salaries and position. They have thus become the chief propagators of the state's socio-religious message. The rule of the Al-Saud family is portrayed in terms of communal stability and religious piety. It is these values that are held in high regard and that are set against the secular values of representative institutions.

The growth and institutionalization of patrimonialism and political culture at the national level are a remarkable adaptation of tradition, harnessing it for the benefit of the modern state. The success of this process can be measured partly by the fact that the new Saudi elites have made substantial personal achievements but have not developed a political programme from which to challenge the monopoly of the traditional ruling class over decision-making. Nevertheless, when considering the attitudes of the younger generations in society one needs to ask how the moral concepts that underpin patronage and charity have been transmitted to the youth. How are such values used by people to assess the political significance of recent financial constraints? In the present situation, the patrimony of the ruling family has become restricted. The effect of this has been to exclude a growing section of the population from the immediate benefits of state largesse.

The tribal, hierarchical order is still functioning. However, the economic decline of the 1980s and 1990s has resulted in restricted state budgets and hence fewer resources to distribute among the middle class. Consequently, tensions have grown between the middle class and the extended royal family. The omnipresent nature of the Saudi state means that its actions are crucial to all those who live within its borders. After almost 50 years of oil-driven state benefits, the population in general have stopped seeing them as a kind gift exchangeable for loyalty to the ruler and now

[6] Madawi Al-Rasheed and Loulouwa Al-Rasheed, 'The Politics of Encapsulation: Saudi Policy Towards Tribal and Religious Opposition', *Middle Eastern Studies*, Vol. 32, No. 1, January 1996, p. 115.

see them as a right of citizenship. According to William Rugh, the Saudi members of the new middle class are ambitious to move up the economic ladder.[7] This ambition distinguishes them from an older generation who had a more fatalistic attitude, which is still common among the population as a whole. At both personal and state level the growth of a professional, ambitious middle class has resulted in an increasing demand for state accountability.

The pressure of the middle class has outrun the ability or economic capacity of the state to find jobs for all of its members. Also, there are limits on the state's ability to find the resources it needs to meet increasing demands for redistribution. Tax follows the pattern of *zakat* (religious obligation), an obligatory alms tax of 2.5 per cent of surplus wealth per annum. The issue of income tax remains a controversial one because *zakat* is considered the only legitimate form of tax according to Islamic law.

The interviews

The interviews were conducted to obtain data on the new middle-class attitudes towards national integrity, power and authority. The responses given revolve around the issue of the moral basis for authority with regard to the exercise of power within the national community. There are seven aspects of this issue that are worth considering in greater detail: the state of the nation; relations with external peoples and powers; divisions within the nation; the moral standing of the state; the place of censorship in Saudi life; the relation of Islam to Saudi life; and the call for modern 'radical' solutions.

The state of the nation

Assessments of the state of the nation among those interviewed show that they see it in terms of both its moral standing and its economic wellbeing, but how people relate these two dimensions is quite varied. Like many others, Naif (23) described the constant decrease in living standards of his generation as miserable and believed that the situation would keep on

[7] William Rugh, 'The Emergence of a New Middle Class in Saudi Arabia'.

deteriorating. He was not, however, referring solely, or even primarily, to material goods such as cars or telephones. He said that material rewards distracted people from reality by focusing attention on buying new cars rather than thinking about serious issues such as politics. For Naif, a materialistic approach to life is compensation for the loss of more valuable but less tangible goods. But he also believes that 'the material-istic approach will lead to a disaster in our country'.

For others the sense of decline is expressed in dramatic terms. Said (27), from a rural tribal background, declares that the government is losing control and the situation is approaching crisis.

Sami (30), from Jeddah, sees things in a different way. Among society's problems that he has observed since returning from studying in the United States is the fact that 'we have no control over basic necessities. Living standards can be maintained by this generation only if they – the authorities – do not censor us.' For those like Sami, having access to material goods is of primary importance, and developing markets is regarded as a key goal.

For yet others there is a strong connection between the economic and moral arguments. Faiz (16), from Ahsa, says that 'we have to become independent of America. We will continue relations because the United States needs the oil and we need the technology, but we need our own factories.' For those like Faiz, national pride rests on being able to exercise national autonomy. For such autonomy to be achieved economic independence is essential.

Not everyone shares this diagnosis. Indeed, relations with people outside the country can be seen in a positive light when contrasted with divisions within Saudi society. Rasha (27) puts this in the starkest of terms: 'Saudis are racist; divisions are based on regions more than on tribes. Nejdis still look down on Hijazis and vice versa. Saudi Arabia is making better progress with external rather than with internal affairs. Internally we have problems.'

Finally, the problem of authority is related to a wider sense of moral decline. Malak (17), from Jeddah, declares that

> problems in society are many. People who have the *sulta* (authority) do nothing about these problems. There is corruption, drugs, drink. There needs to be a much closer relation between what is demanded by Islam

and what is enshrined in law. *Shari'a* (Islamic law) should be implemented equally for everyone, but first and foremost on the political leaders themselves.

Foreign relations

The strongly articulated sense of moral decline expressed by contemporary youth is frequently voiced alongside criticism of the relations between Saudi Arabia and Western powers, especially the United States of America. There has been a marked shift away from the relatively open and relaxed view of the United States common in the 1970s. The attitudes expressed above by Faiz are now widespread amongst the new generation. For instance, Youssef (15) from Ras Tannoura, echoes Faiz's view when he says 'we must get rid of the Americans and do things ourselves. If we have no oil they will not deal with us.' Youssef, like many other young Saudis, feels that the country is vulnerable and over-dependent on America. His mistrust is not based on overtly Islamist/anti-Western ideas but rather on national pride. It is his opinion that his country would act differently if it were not tied so closely to the United States.

Another significant strand of thought hostile towards the existing relations between Saudi Arabia and the United States is more clearly couched in terms of cultural values. For instance, Haifa (16), from Riyadh, shares the belief that the economic tie to the United States is detrimental to her nation. 'Petrol has been the means by which the Americans manipulated us. Saudi Arabia gave America too much, more than it should have taken.' However, Haifa is concerned more explicitly about her country from an Islamic perspective. She believes that the Americans are a threat to Saudi Arabia's religious and national identity. Abdul Aziz (30), from Jeddah, expresses deep-seated concerns about the influence of America: 'The United States is doing its best to ruin our country; it is doing its best to rule us. They are trying their best to corrupt our Islamic identity.' For these young people it is not simply a matter of autonomy; rather, it is a matter of cultural integrity.

The idea that Westerners enjoy forms of favouritism finds expression in various ways. For instance, Abdul Aziz claims that foreigners, especially Americans, have advantages over others in the salary system (even for the same profession) and legal discrimination is rife as regards non-Western, especially non-American expatriates. If an American and an ordinary Saudi commit the same offence, the Saudi with no *wasta* (family connections) is more harshly punished.

In their interviews most young people said relations with the United States were a constraint on the development of a more clearly articulated and distinct sense of cultural identity. However, they did not articulate their disquiet in geopolitical terms. Rather, as will be seen below, they couched criticisms of their rulers in personal terms. Their political elites were seen as beholden to the United States or else led astray by their relations with them. This is sharply expressed by Hamad (29), from a southern tribe:

The Americans are thieves who are stealing our money, money that we need for our own people, and this is the biggest puzzle. How are they allowed to rob us like this? What is our government's relationship with the United States? We went to ask the princes about this ambiguity but they have nothing to say. We are a colonized country, colonized by the United States of America.

In order to develop a cultural identity these members of the new generation believed greater contact with the non-American world beyond national boundaries, especially with the other member countries of the regional GCC, to be crucial.

Since the early 1980s, there have been major changes in the identity and allegiances of the population across the GCC area. In Saudi Arabia itself, the regime has encouraged the reduction of regional loyalties while it has furthered the centralization of the state. Also since 1981 the formation of the GCC has hastened the creation of a regional Gulf Arab identity. This process has been encouraged by a sense of vulnerability that is shared across the region. Caught between their two larger and unpredictable neighbours, Iran and Iraq, the populations of the GCC have formed ties of solidarity that work both above and below official government ties. This has resulted in the emergence of a recognizable 'Gulf culture', tribally and Islamically based and identifiable in dress, music and specific gender distinctions. This trend has been encouraged by the increasing rates of intermarriage across the region, especially among those of 'tribal' origins. Administratively, this trend has been encouraged by a new approach to passport control. Travellers holding GCC passports are processed separately and more quickly than those from other Arab and Muslim countries. Thus, the new generation is the first to see itself as part of this emerging group which was not talked about before 1981. The emerging 'Gulf identity' does not include the entire Gulf region. In particular the two major powers, Arab Iraq and non-Arab Iran, are excluded. When I asked Jassem (23) about relations with neighbouring Muslim countries such as Iran, he said, 'No, we are not allowed to go there. It has been stamped in our passports alongside Israel.'

Divisions within Saudi society

The importance of personal relations with respect to the way in which politics works is a reality about which most young people are keenly aware. The moral basis of economic life in their grandparents' era relied heavily on personal ties of one kind or another. Those in positions of power and authority were expected to use their role and command over social wealth to ensure the relative wellbeing of the community as a whole. It was to such people that those in need would turn in times of trouble. With both tribal and family relations retaining such importance in Saudi Arabia, the importance of the personal has by no means disappeared. Indeed, having a personal tie to the top of the state elite is still the best way to get things done in any Gulf state. However, for various reasons this is not an option open to all. For one thing, a larger population, fuelled by high birth rates in all Gulf monarchies, means that an ever smaller percentage of the population can claim to have a direct personal tie. Another factor is the sheer growth in the importance of the state to the everyday lives of ordinary people. In many ways, the state supplemented the patrimonial ties of the previous order.

The scale and complexity of urbanized life in Saudi Arabia mean that social relations have changed substantially. A key feature of this change is the distance between the rulers and the ruled. Samir (15), from Hail, captures this sense of distance in the following way: 'In the past a man went to the King for "complaints". Today this is no longer possible, but the princes still help people, not the King.' Although Samir believes that a change has occurred in the patrimony of the ruling elite, he still has hope in the younger princes, who are educated and accessible and who could help the people.

These kinds of divisions have an impact on everyday life. In Saudi society the state is all-pervasive, and access to goods and services often depends on the nature of one's personal ties with figures in authority. One's personal, family and tribal connections can be of tremendous importance as a result. For those who lack the right contacts, access to goods and services can be difficult. Sami, for instance, complains that 'we cannot get mobile phones unless we have *wasta*. If the water is cut off from your home, it cannot be fixed without *wasta*. Things that you take for granted abroad, we don't have here, so the average person suffers.' Omar (16), from Jeddah, thinks that welfare is not evenly distributed for all citizens: 'I would not get what others will if I receive 2,000 riyals and others 5,000. All this depends on the class and tribe of the person.' He believes that Saudi society should not be divided by tribalism: 'All Saudi Arabians should unite.' Omar also wants more equality and more civil rights for Saudi citizens. This demand for equality and civil rights is more precisely defined in the mind of Hamad:

> There is a big discrepancy between north and south. I am from the south, and we are trying to take care of the poor and keep a school in the village of al-Baha. Those who live in Jeddah or Dammam don't feel these problems. Even the roads in the south have many accidents. There is a road where I come from called the road of death because the government does not spend on bettering the conditions of rural areas. Hail and Qasim also do not have services, not even one-fifth of what exists in other areas.

Inevitably, the role played by the state puts the country's rulers in a difficult position. Direct state control of social resources, and indirect control of resources in the private hands of the ruling family, means that people will be quick to blame the ruling elite when times get harder.

The moral standing of the state

In many people's remarks, there was a close association between problems of government control and the moral standing of some of those associated with government. Sami, for instance, put it this way: 'The problem here is that the government controls everything.' Said blames the government for using its position to foster the *ittikali* (rentier mentality). These men from quite different backgrounds see the current system as failing to meet their expectations. The state encourages dependence, but it does not fulfil its obligations to those who look to it for their needs.

For others of the new generation, there are failings in different areas of life. Faiz says that he is concerned about domestic security following bombings and other attempted acts of terrorism. He says that

> they – the government – are not learning the lesson. They have a laid-back attitude … When I visited the Great Mosque in Mecca, there was not enough security. This relaxed approach to security is matched by laxity is other areas. There is no consistency in the law, and penalties that are set should be respected. The satellite [dish] is illegal but the king has the biggest satellite in Mecca.

As noted above, Malak sees the problem of elite hypocrisy in even stronger terms. Her explanation for why bad things happen is that 'the government themselves do it. The authorities themselves are drug users. They should have more fear of God. On the one hand they pray but on the other they pick up the bottle.'

The place of censorship in Saudi life

Opinions on censorship provide more evidence of attitudes towards authority. These are generally of three kinds. What might be called more conservative opinion holds that it is the role of government to help to sustain the moral values of the community, and that it should be left to the elites to make decisions about these matters. At the same time, many of the same people believe the government has failed to uphold such values and also that the law fails to reflect the views of the majority when it comes to such matters. What could be called more liberal opinion sees censorship as a kind of barrier between the people and the state. For these people some liberalization of restrictions would lead to greater trust and better understanding.

Adnan (24), from Mecca, accepts that government can be right to maintain certain kinds of restriction. She thinks that censorship is a way of protecting values; it gives security to the government. In a similar vein, Salman (25), from Ahsa, accepted that 'censorship in Saudi Arabia should be a compromise. What is available in Saudi Arabia compared to what is available in Britain are the two extremes. Some freedom of expression is necessary for progress, but this cannot be unrestrained.' Salman is not convinced that the Saudi population want to be consulted by government. He thinks that many people are happy to let the government do what it does best. Nor is he convinced that greater democracy necessarily would be a good thing. He argues that the extent of tribal links means that there can be no proper democracy.

A positive attitude towards a more inclusive, democratic approach is supported by Mansour (30). He too thinks that censorship is sometimes necessary, but he adds the qualification that it has to be intelligent censorship. He thinks that freedom of expression is necessary but has to go hand in hand with *taw'ia* (enlightenment). Mansour clearly expresses the idea that both rulers and ruled should act morally and responsibly, and that certain forms of government censorship can promote socially responsible attitudes. Majid (23) develops this approach further. He argues against censorship on the grounds that it encourages distrust between the people and their rulers:

> It is forbidden by royal decree to have a satellite dish, but if you go to 30th Street you find a display of dishes everywhere, or if you go from the airport throughout the city, on the whole things are only allowed for the Al-Saud. When we know the reason our amazement will disappear, but forbidding things without us knowing why is not good.

Abdul Ilah (23) also wants to see better relations established between rulers and ruled, and he complains about excessive censorship:

> Politics and economics are taboo subjects. I am not allowed to express my opinion, except in trivialities, although anything that happens in

the country concerns me because I am concerned with building my society. No one takes my opinion.

Ahmed (21) also thinks that censorship in Saudi society is not beneficial in terms of protecting Saudi values; instead 'it only contributes to evading the truth'. He thinks freedom of expression is necessary for progress, but it should be defined according to time and place.

Abdul Rahman (18), from Riyadh, liked the idea of becoming a minister and introducing changes. When asked about the possible decline in living standards of the young relative to that of their parents he replied that 'we first want to know our assets. We are not clearly told by our governments what we have and what we don't.' He does not believe in censorship and does not think it is beneficial for Saudi society. He believes that freedom of expression is necessary for progress. Sahar (30), from Jeddah, is more forthright: 'Censorship, it is hated by everybody.' For her it only reflects the fear of the authorities. She also thinks that freedom of expression is related to progress. Yassir (22) shares this view: 'Censorship is a problem in Saudi Arabia. There are too many limitations on what people should see and comment on, and people are starting to feel the constraints.' Fahad (23) says that 'there is too much censorship in Saudi Arabia. For example, if a woman is wearing a short skirt, they cut her out of the film.'

The relationship of Islam to Saudi political life

The new generation's attitudes towards censorship are expressive of a growing lack of deference towards authority and a stronger democratic sensibility. This is democratic in the sense that ordinary people do not have to take their ruler's statements at face value but are instead likely to take a more independent stance. Something very similar could be said in respect of Islam. There is very little questioning of the value of Islam *per se*. The interviewees considered themselves good Muslims. The democratic aspect is to be found in the range of interpretations of Islam and in attitudes of questioning, even hostility, towards the religious and political establishment. The adherence to Islam comes across in the criticisms levelled at what is regarded as the hypocrisy of the ruling elite.

Dana (15) says that religious extremism is bad and that the *mutaw'a* are bad for society. These views were shared by many of those who also argued for a more tolerant attitude towards censorship. This rarely, however, implied an anti-Islamic view. Sahar's rejection of the current system of censorship also expressed the gap between the requirements of Islam and the behaviour of the rulers. Censorship, she argued, 'has nothing to do with our values'.

Jamila, Asia, Amel and Ahlam, from Jeddah, have pointed out some of the inconsistencies in government practices, and that the contradictions stem from weaknesses *vis-à-vis* religion and the demands of the people. They gave as an example the use of *riba* (financial interest), which is forbidden by the *mashaikh* (religious authorities) and practised by the government. They are critical of the political leadership and believe that there are two laws in the country – one for the ruled and one for the rulers. They are for greater equality, greater cohesion and more Islamic consistency. These four young women had studied throughout their lives in Saudi Arabia, not abroad. Nevertheless, debates that touch on political issues are becoming more normal at university level, especially for the children of the educated class.

Faiz highlighted what he saw as the differences between Islam and the current legal system. He went a good deal further than pointing out the inconsistencies in the system. It was not the Islamic character of government, but its absence, that he criticized. 'The government is not Islamic, monarchy is not Islamic, forbidding women not to drive is not Islamic.' Faiz is more rebellious than many others, perhaps owing to his wealthy background and his extended exposure to the United States as a student. He is relatively more politicized than many others, although he does not have a clear definition of the character of political power in his society.

For the majority of the interviewees, a greater adherence to the values of Islam and respect for members of the national community would change society for the better. For others, it demanded a more committed approach to one's religion. Layla (15) declared that 'people should fight for their freedom'. She believes that in a situation where the state acts as the guardian of Islam, it should not be so rigid, or inconsistent. 'In Saudi Arabia they make everything *haram* (religiously forbidden) for us [meaning citizens] while it is *halal* (religiously approved) for them [meaning the authorities].' For many others this entailed a more open society in which matters of public concern could be discussed more freely. For some the idea of openness entailed a move towards more Western-style institutions. Faiz, for instance, argued that for Saudi Arabia to become a part of global society it needs to open its borders and abolish strict social rules; people must be given more opportunities. Even this, however, was seen as conforming to Islam: 'Everything is justified by Islam,' he said.

Radical solutions

Although the experience of contact with Western society, most notably in the shape of the United States, is regarded with increasing suspicion and hostility, there are those who call for the introduction of Western institutions into Saudi Arabian society and who find the liberal, secular institutions of free markets and political rights particularly attractive. Like others educated abroad, Sami (30) had the opportunity to make comparisons with the West because of his exposure as a student to another culture. He believes that civil rights are lacking in Saudi Arabia compared with other countries where people are guaranteed rights and protection by law. Sami's discovery of the concept of individual rights has led him to develop high expectations. He is also disappointed that he is not rewarded for his education by promotion to a higher-paying job, but he still has mixed feelings and ideas. He expresses frustration but not coherent political ideas. Sami thinks that 'the problem here is that the government controls everything and we need to develop the private sector'. His solution to the overpowering role of the state is to develop the market as an alternative source of goods and services.

Radical institutional change was believed necessary by others, most usually those who had direct experience of the West. Naif argued for republicanism: 'Throughout history, industrialization under a monarchy has not been proper. For industry you shouldn't have a monarchy. Unless there is a movement that will change the present system, no progress will be made.' Saad (16), from Taif, argued that the changes had to go much deeper: 'Saudi society had every type of revolution except the social. It had an agricultural and an economic revolution, but people's mentality did not change. We have reached a stage where we must have a social revolution.' Saad's opinions are more outspoken than the majority of those interviewed. He lived for two years in England and he comes from a more liberal background. Sami too argued for radical change: 'We are willing to fight, but we are limited by tribal and religious traditions. *Al-taqalid la tismah* (traditions do not permit).'

Conclusion

Over the last two generations national political culture in Saudi Arabia has developed the category of the 'traditional,' a category which is central to how the new generation understands the nature of the society in which it lives. This conception of a 'traditional' world separate from and unaffected by rapid economic change provides a basis for dealing with the processes and problems of modernization. As economic insecurity becomes a key factor in the new generation's lives a heightened perception of what has been taken away in the transformation of Saudi society is detectable. Naif's criticism of the emptiness of an increasingly material life is widely echoed amongst the new generation. The negative aspects of 'modernity' or 'globalization' are generally blamed on easily identifiable targets such as the Americans and the culture they appear to bring into the country. Saudi 'tradition' for the new generation is becoming a way of developing a moral and political critique of the West but also of the government's apparent dependence upon America.

The development of the category of tradition does not mean that there is not self-consciously 'modern', class-based, functional, ideological and more secular thinking. The undoubted importance of a romanticized construction of the past is evidence of the confusing and all-embracing pace of societal transformation. Chambers of commerce, on the other hand, are the most prominent example of organizations championing the call for 'modern' reforms and for a greater scope for market economics.[8] Chambers of commerce have allowed common interests to develop among their members, as a direct result of societal transformation.[9] Professional syndicates give an identity to business people that is non-tribal and has a degree of independence from direct state patronage. This

[8] See Gregory F. Gause, *Oil Monarchies, Domestic and Security Challenges in the Arab Gulf States* (New York: Council on Foreign Relations Press, 1994), p. 87.
[9] Ibid.

allows these groups the political space to formulate demands for political authority to be made subject to greater accountability. The very category of the 'new generation' is an example of such a process. These young people have a conscious collective image of themselves as a nationwide and even an inter-state Gulf grouping with an identity separate from and above sub-state groupings such as tribe or region. Members of the new generation, in expressing their views forcibly, are calling for change in the name of a national group which should be recognized and listened to. However, there is little evidence as yet that these groups – whether the new generation, the new middle class or members of professional organizations – are the nucleus of any coherent movement for political reform. But in the medium to long run the growth of nationwide identities will give rise to increasing calls for accountability and reform.

It is within the shared political culture that both rulers and ruled seek to understand how their world has been transformed and what this means for their present and future lives. The Saudi Arabian state, more than others in the region, has attempted to adapt the traditional social and moral practices of Islam to the new conditions and role of a modern state. The use of Islam to do this has, however, become a double-edged sword. Although it has provided a set of unifying cultural symbols, it has also produced a vocabulary that can be deployed to criticize the ruling elite and call for a change in the direction of government policy. Such demands are hard for the state to crack down on because they are framed in the same terms as the language the state uses to legitimate itself. The government is caught between two broad sections of the new generation with different perceptions of the role of religion within society. Those who graduated from *shari'a* colleges, largely rural in family origin and alienated from the urban Saudi Arabia that personifies change, have mastered the language of Islamic legitimacy and have the potential to turn it against the state. 'With limited room for political expression, religious life remains an open avenue for dissent.'[10] The second section, influenced by the role of Islam in other, more secular Middle Eastern states, sees the Saudi state's attitude to religion as repressive and outdated. For these young people Islam is a part of their everyday lives but they want the right to decide which part and how to incorporate their belief into their role as Saudi citizens.

[10] Joseph Kechichian, 'Islamic Revivalism and the Change in Saudi Arabia: Juhayman-Al-Utaybi's "Letters" to the Saudi People,' *The Muslim World*, Vol. LXXX, No. 1, January 1990, p. 3.

Mordechai Abir argues that

> the distinction made by the Saudi 'lower class' between *hukuma* and *dawla*, both of which they commonly take to mean government, is significant for the nature of Saudi political culture. To the average Saudi, *dawla* is used to describe the modern central government and its agencies, largely controlled by Western-educated bureaucrats of urban origin. The development of the central government and the expansion of its services and rapid urbanization bought the Saudi middle and lower classes, both largely of Bedouin origin, into daily contact with the *dawla* and made them dependent on services and subsidies provided by it. There is a wide-spread alienation amongst these new townspeople. They see the bureaucrats on whom they depend as inferior and crafty. These civil servants in return show little respect to those who have not mastered the bureaucratic system. ... In opposition to *dawla* the new townspeople identify the paternalistic notion of *hukuma* with personal contact, respect and an understanding of their problems. The notion of *hukuma* is attached to a paternalistic government. This perception of government is above the cold functionality of the bureaucrats. It is more comparable to an understanding of what is 'traditional', it supplies their needs in a manner which is perceived as Saudi and not a foreign-inspired aberration.[11]

This idealized understanding of the role of the ruling family juxtaposed against the actions of the bureaucracy is being transformed by the lack of government resources and perceptions of increased corruption. For many, the idea of *hukuma* is no longer to be found among the distant and aloof ruling elite, who have become more *dawla* in recent years. What was once a distinction between the honourable ruler and his devious advisers has become the new distinction between an ideal set of moral standards by which all political authority should be judged and the practical activities of the rulers which fall short of this.

For the new generation these idealized standards are a mixture of old ideas of what personalized rule should be and new meritocratic ideals of equal access and efficient government. Whereas Samir (15), from Hail,

[11] Mordechai Abir, 'The Consolidation of the Ruling Class and the New Elites in Saudi Arabia', p. 164.

sees the young princes as *hukuma* when compared to the king, the reasons for this designation show the transformation of the concept. The princes are accessible because they are young and educated abroad. There is empathy between them and the other members of the new generation because they share a common set of experiences and a new or at least partially transformed approach to life. The division between the new generation and the princes on one side and the old ruling elite on the other is partly understood as a division between a more 'modern' or 'fair' approach to government on one side and an unchanged and possibly unsustainable one on the other.

Much of Western political theory revolves around the distinction between markets and states. For the tradition from Hobbes to Hegel[12] and beyond, the market has been seen as a place of unrestrained private ambition.[13] This tradition sees the state as necessary for social cohesion. It is this understanding of the state that the Saudi Arabian ruling elite deploy. The nation needs to be defended from external dangers as well as internal ones. The state brings guidance, prosperity but crucially stability. The dangers associated with this view have been identified by the more politically aware among the new generation. While the state watches over society, there is no one left to watch over the state.

The rival tradition of thought sees the market, or civil society, as the locus of association, as the place where people acquire a sense of the political. It is through their active participation in civil associations that people acquire the power of collective action and amplify their voice, thus restraining government action. Tocqueville, for instance, sees the art of association as the mother of all action. 'An association unites the efforts of minds which have a tendency to diverge, in one single channel, and urges them vigorously towards one single end which it points out.'[14] Tocqueville sees civil associations as arenas in which individuals can direct their attention to more than their selfish, conflictual, narrowly private goals. Through their activities in civil associations, they come to perceive that they are not independent of their fellow citizens and that in

[12] G.W. F. Hegel, *Philosophy of Right*, translated by T.H. Knox (London/New York: Oxford University Press, 1967), p. 339.
[13] John Keane (ed.), *Civil Society and the State: New European Perspectives* (London/New York: Verso, 1988), p. 51.
[14] Tocqueville, Alexis Charles de, *Democracy in America*, Vol. 2, (New York: Henri Maurice Clirel and J. & H.G. Langley, 1845) p. 220.

order to obtain others' support they often must lend them their cooperation.

It is this view, the one that recognizes the crucial separation between
the state on one side and civil society and the market on the other, that
increasingly informs the ideas of a large section of the new generation. In
criticizing state intervention in religious matters and censorship they are
implicitly calling for constraint on state power. Society itself and,
crucially, the young and educated members of society must have the
autonomy to choose what path they take. This is not a call for the
diminution of the role Islam plays in society. Nor are young people trying
to dispense with tradition and the place it has in guaranteeing stability;
what they are increasingly calling for is the space, both politically and
socially, to choose what is best for themselves. The incoherent criticisms
of government, corruption and double standards are slowly forming into
a call not for revolt but for more autonomy to pursue the goals that their
education and experiences have led them to expect.

3 Education

Encountering globalization and restructuring tradition

Family and education represent two often conflicting sources of socialization in a rapidly changing society. Education has been one of the major vehicles for the transmission of external values and is bound to have an uneasy relationship with existing social and familial standards. A society that attempts to tame globalization and to control change through the variety of choice provided in education is risking conflict with existing traditional institutions.

The educational choices available for the new generation in Saudi Arabia are much more varied than at any point in the past. With the recent proliferation of private schools, the new middle class has a wider choice of modern non-religious education, with curricula changing to be more compatible with the demands of the outside world. Those of the new generation interviewed are aware that the problem is no longer purely the availability of education but rather its relevance to modern requirements, to their welfare and future careers. In other words, it is the quality rather than the quantity of education that is the main issue for them.

In Saudi Arabia there is an intricate hierarchy of prestige regarding the subject area of degree study and training programmes. Whether educated at home or abroad, young people have been socialized to consider certain categories of studies more acceptable than others; certain disciplines, especially medicine, are regarded as 'honourable' and as such are unique status symbols. Those who take such courses, both men and women, even at domestic universities, garner social cachet over and above career advancement and monetary rewards.

This socially determined attitude to education persists despite being under siege owing to economic hardship and a globalizing culture of modernity. Against the backdrop of increasing choice and competition to secure education and employment, members of the new generation make no effort to hide their admiration for the traditional knowledge of their forefathers or the relative ease and financial security of the life-style that was characteristic of their parents' generation. However, it is indicative of future trends and present insecurities that employment problems led several young male interviewees to state that their educational choices will no longer be driven by prestige alone. Obtaining training that will help them acquire professional expertise and increase their chances of winning secure employment has now become a key concern. This is true not only for the middle class but also for the elite who in the absence of the economic boom of the previous decades rely increasingly on education to secure and maintain their status in Saudi society. Against this background, the majority of all Saudi youth, no matter what their social background, still believe it is a right to go on to further education and to university. This belief in educational entitlement appears to be, in some cases, disconnected from educational achievement or commitment to study. Some see a disjunction between what they aspire to and the reality of the educational curriculum, and between their ambitions and their socio-economic environment. Those who undertook higher education remain frustrated, complaining that the present does not provide for their professional, political and social expectations and potential.

Most interviewees, both those educated at home and those who have studied abroad, expressed the desire to return and settle in Saudi Arabia once their training had finished and their careers had been established. The choice to return for the majority was unquestioned. This points first to a growth in a Saudi nationalism that was only born in the parents' generation. It also highlights a sense of incoherence and dislocation. The new generation has grown up in a complex, confusing and rapidly changing world. Its members return to Saudi Arabia to deploy the learning and skills they have acquired from a Western-style curriculum and institutions for the benefit of their community. However, they also return in search of a sense of certainty and belonging; they may want to change Saudi Arabia but they still seek out a society that has continuity with the past, a country which they recognize and in which they feel at home. Their social identity and status are defined at home in relation to others in the community. Foreign education is adapted and serves to enhance status and identity.

Nevertheless, with respect to the development of the new generation's sense of identity, the family/education and the tradition/modernity divide have created contradictions and ambiguities. The interviewees make a distinction between the road to learning undertaken in Saudi educational establishments and an 'inquiring mind' which they either develop independently or acquire from non-Saudis. They believe that a truly independent approach to knowledge, a questioning approach, is gained through contact with outside influences such as travel or from foreign teachers (Egyptian, Lebanese and Jordanian). However, in an attempt to retain cultural coherence and to maintain contact with their own culture, they remain apprehensive about Western teachers in Saudi Arabia, despite the fact that most of them aspire to study in Western countries. Suhair (27), for example, argued that the Saudi university curriculum does not compete with the outside world. The introduction of change, she said is *lazem* (a must) at the university level. The curricula are nothing but *hashu* (stuffing): 'We have to change because the curricula emphasize the memorization of facts, and this memorization is repeated from one year to another. They produce generations of *hashu*, and these generations cannot compare with those of Jordan or Lebanon.' She also stated that Saudis should rely more on foreign guidance to improve educational standards, especially at university level.

The historical development of the Saudi Arabian education system

The interviewees were aware of the vast developments in the educational system since the days of their grandparents and realize that great progress has been achieved. Modern secular forms of education were the exception prior to the unification of Saudi Arabia in the 1930s. In the urban Hijaz, education for boys took place within the framework of the *'ulama,* religious scholarly circles in mosques, especially the Great Mosque of Mecca. The first secular school in Jeddah opened in 1903 under the name *falah* (success); another was established two years later in Mecca under the same name. These schools were for men only. During this period girls received traditional forms of education at home or at the *kuttab*. The first state schools for men opened only after the unification of the Kingdom of Saudi Arabia.

Women gained the right to attend schools by a royal decree in 1959. The first secular schools for girls opened in Jeddah in the early 1960s, the very first being *dar al-hanan* (House of Tenderness), sponsored by Iffat, King Faisal's wife.[1] The objectives *of dar al-hanan* were described as being to produce better mothers and home-makers through Islamic-guided instruction. The popular saying that 'the Mother can be a school in herself if you prepare her well' featured prominently in school books. This motto was necessary to persuade the religious establishment that women's education supported religion and tradition rather than deviating from it. During the 1960s other private schools for girls were set up: *riyadh al-atfal* (The Oasis of Children), directed by a Lebanese woman, and *rawdat al-ma'aref* (The Garden of Knowledge), directed by a Palestinian woman. Both schools are sponsored by female royal patrons.

Between the late 1950s and the 1970s, it was possible for the more affluent in Saudi Arabia to send their children, both sons and daughters, to study abroad, mostly in other Arab countries or in Europe and the United States. This trend increased as a result of the great wealth acquired in the boom conditions of the 1970s. Women of the merchant and educated classes during that period pursued higher education and several obtained university degrees from foreign universities.

During the 1980s, a period characterized by the prevailing moods of 'piety' and 'tradition', the desire or pressure to conform to strict Saudi Islamic behaviour and cultural propriety was more pronounced.[2] The 1980s were a period of consolidation compared with the previous two decades of openness to change. Accordingly, social trends changed to emphasize study at domestic institutions rather than abroad. This followed the incident in the Great Mosque in 1979 when Juhaiman Al-Utaybi led a group of Islamic radicals in a demonstration, as well as the Iranian Islamic revolution. A contributing factor, of course, was the need to reduce expenditure in the emerging context of a less favourable economic climate and the increasing demographic pressures.

[1] See Ibtissam A. Al-Bassam, 'Institutions of Higher Education for Women in Saudi Arabia', *International Journal of Educational Development*, Vol. 4, No. 3, 1984, pp. 255–8.
[2] See Mai Yamani, 'Formality and Propriety in the Hijaz', unpublished PhD thesis, Oxford University, 1990.

A positive result of such trends was the much improved standards of Saudi schools compared with two decades earlier. Subjects such as computing and modern languages became central to the expanding curriculum. The three reinforcing trends of 'piety', economy and educational development led to a growing reluctance on the part of parents to educate their children in the West. In the late 1970s the government reduced the number of scholarships offered to Saudis, specifically discouraging Saudi women from studying abroad unless accompanied by their guardians, i.e. their husbands or fathers. This resulted in a large increase in the numbers of women enrolling in universities in the main cities of Saudi Arabia.

Although the 1980s witnessed a huge expansion of mass education, at the same time there was a concomitant increase in the control by the *'ulama*. The *'ulama's* influence started to shape what could be taught at universities and how women in higher education should be supervised; for example, women were barred from studying subjects such as engineering and law and a strict gender segregation was maintained in all educational spheres.

Nevertheless, in today's Saudi Arabia most women under the age of thirty have some experience of modern schooling, including university education. They read newspapers and magazines; some read novels, local and foreign. However, for most women higher education still does not lead to a career. The justification for universal access to education is considered part of Islamic teachings. Primary education is compulsory and has led to high literacy rates for both sexes. Women often resort to quoting from the Prophet's *hadith* in order to support their desire to learn: 'Seek knowledge from the cradle to the grave', and 'Seek knowledge even from China'.

As Saudi government funding became increasingly restricted from the mid-1980s, educational programmes began to shift the emphasis from higher education to specialized skills for the labour market. This has been linked to the provision of more opportunities for women. In accordance with the government's stated aim of greater economic diversification and indigenization, more emphasis has been placed on these types of technical schools in order to meet the demands of restructuring. In the area of technical education, there are already three institutes of technology, one model agricultural institute, 44 vocational training centres and a host of other schools.

The rise in those entering higher education during the 1970s and 1980s was meant to provide the personnel for the Saudi-ization of state industries and the bureaucracy. However, because an estimated 25 per cent of students graduate from Islamic universities, this has led to a pool of graduates not immediately employable in the wider public sector. Most young men from the new middle class express doubts about the correlation between progress and studying at Islamic colleges. In group interviews, they cited the fate of relatives who had studied at Islamic colleges but were unable to find jobs related to their studies. In this context, Samir (15) exclaimed: 'What's the use of studying a subject if you are going to be employed in a totally different field? And that [employment], of course, would have to do with whether you have *wasta* or not.'

During the 1990s, the trend of educating children at tertiary level in Saudi Arabia decreased. Those with wealth or access to government largesse began again to send children abroad in increasing numbers, especially to the United States. Those who can afford private education for their offspring have opted for 'modern' education, which they believe is only available overseas. Such education brings with it a much valued proficiency in English. The royal family, and the political, merchant and educated classes, all educate their sons and daughters abroad. The practice is even favoured by the more conservative Islamists. However, it remains more of a privilege for sons than daughters, except in the most liberal of households. Most families wishing to send their children abroad wait until they have completed the ninth year of schooling so that they gain a strong sense of Saudi-Islamic culture. Others leave for university education only after having completed their secondary schooling in Saudi Arabia.

Educational values and the new generation

Family influence

The family has traditionally been the main institution of socialization in Saudi Arabia. The family also represents the key arena for the conflict between what are seen as the influences of modernization and the certainties of tradition. The parents of the new generation push their children

to obtain from education all the advantages that training and qualifications can bring. However, education, whether in Saudi Arabia or
abroad, can also bring with it challenging and unsettling views.

For the new generation, despite the influence of education and the
media, the institution of the family remains the key point of reference.
The majority of the young people interviewed said that their families had
influenced their attitudes and personalities more than their education.
Most expressed respect for their father's education and occupation, and
their career options were heavily influenced by their parents' wishes and
experiences. Although some young people expressed frustration about
their families' constraining influence on educational choices, the majority used the experiences and opinions of key family members to choose
the discipline they studied and the career training they undertook.

Abdul Rahman (18) is clearly from a wealthy and influential family.
This allowed him to be educated at *madaris najd*, one of the two best
private boys' schools in Riyadh. After he left *madaris najd* it was still
thought necessary to send him for one year to a private school in the
United States. This, he said, was in order to strengthen his English
language and academic skills. Abdul Rahman is now a first-year business
studies undergraduate at an American university. He seemed unsure why
he chose this specific course. When asked the reason, he replied vaguely:
'because business is important'. After further thought he said that his
family encouraged his choice of study.

Many of the older interviewees obtained degrees similar to those of their
fathers in the hope of joining the family business or taking up a similar
career. Omar (16) expressed a common theme: 'I want to graduate from
university and work in a company just like my father.' However, there
were some among those interviewed, especially those living in urban
areas, who did not follow this pattern. With the expansion of primary and
secondary education, young Saudis are now experiencing a much more
diverse range of educational influences. Generation by generation, the
educational system has expanded from its primarily religious basis
through a concern with scientific and practical learning to a point where
the arts are now in greater demand in schools. This means that young
people who want to develop such interests feel constrained by the more
conservative example of older family members. For example, Mish'al
(29), from Riyadh, fought a long battle with his parents over which

educational path he should take. Mish'al's father is a doctor, and the family wanted him to enter this prestigious profession. This meant that he was actively discouraged from studying art until the age of eighteen, and had to focus on *'ilmi* (sciences) at the secondary level. Throughout his education in Riyadh, Mish'al found an outlet for his aesthetic interests with a favourite teacher who taught him classical Arabic and Quranic scholarship; through Arabic poetry, for example, he found inspiration that helped his creativity. It was not until he departed for the United States to pursue higher education that he managed to circumvent family aspirations, and he finally graduated in art and design.

Sami (30), from Jeddah, experienced a similar rigidity of family expectations. Sami went to a private school (*al-thaghar*) in Jeddah. He was then sent for two years to the University of Riyadh. His family was determined that he become a doctor like his father. Sami hated medicine, 'loving anything electronic from the age of nine'. But for his family, electronic engineering or computer science could in no way deliver the prestige and social standing of a doctor. Thus, he remained under pressure to study medicine and to stay in Saudi Arabia. However, Sami persisted in his desire to escape a career in medicine and returned from Riyadh to study computer science at the University of Jeddah, after which he went to the United States where he obtained a BSc. Sami's success in avoiding his family's rigid definition of an acceptable career is indicative of the changes sweeping Saudi society.

On a purely practical level, the Saudi government cannot pour resources into state medical provision as it once did. This means public health care has become cash-strapped and services vary according to geographic location. Sami's love of electronics may well enable him to pursue as successful a career as his father in a country that is desperate to expand its manufacturing sector and escape its perceived reliance on the United States for technology transfer. On another level, changes in attitudes towards traditional norms, and especially family authority, are expressed in professional choices. For instance, Faris (16), from Qasim, says that his family background has had a great influence on his attitude and personality. His father, the director of an established Saudi firm, wants him to study law but Faris wants to start training at the Aramco oil company and work with Americans: 'We need more technological advancement in our country.' His view of the difference between his generation and that of his parents is that 'we have the education and the knowledge they did not have, and the children of the poor will be richer'.

The new generation is faced with more choices, which will eventually enable it to outgrow social and familial expectations. This trend is more pronounced for women, who now have options that were not conceivable in their mothers' generation (see Chapter 5). The views of two sisters from the new middle class, Hawazin (15) and Hind (19), give an idea of the doubts and fears of other young people when confronting the future. Although Hawazin has travelled to the United States and the United Kingdom and wants to study medicine, she would prefer to marry a 'rich man' who would provide her with the security she feels she needs. Hind is studying medicine, but cannot contemplate travelling abroad to further her career. The sisters are not from a wealthy background and are critical of the fashionable tastes of wealthier families. Hind says she does not want a lot of servants. Another pair of sisters, Jamila and Asia, from the educated class, have studied at King Abdul Aziz University and the House of Tenderness school, respectively, and complain that the choice of subjects to study is limited. They regret that the authorities restrict their choices and remark in addition that their families are over-protective and do not permit them to travel abroad for further education.

On a more general note, it is clear from the interviews that the family still provides the main reference point for the new generation's identity formation. It is also the main tool for determining the moral and social structures within which Saudi life evolves. Nevertheless, the exposure of Saudi youth to ever more diverse experiences, ranging from the Internet and satellite television to a more secular education system, leads to a perception, shared by their parents, that externally driven change is becoming faster and more uncontrolled. Under these circumstances it is not surprising that what young people demand from their education system and what they then aspire to in their careers is already different from the demands and aspirations of their parents' generation. The generational gap is widening and in a more bewildering way than the change that took place between the grandparents' and the parents' generation.

The need for English

For young Saudi Arabians the ability to speak a foreign language has become a symbol of a range of conflicting aspirations. The grandparents' generation did not speak English. For the parents' generation English became concentrated among government officials of the educated class, while the global economy now demands a widespread proficiency. The English encountered in American-made films has made it the language of modernity, the vehicle of all that is different, exciting and innovative. English has become juxtaposed against Arabic, the sacred language of Islam but also the means of communicating with the elders of the family. This clash has come to be portrayed in a modern/traditional dichotomy. English is also the language of instruction and of technical knowledge, and it is crucial for success in the secular fields of business, commerce, higher education and government. Therefore, proficiency in spoken and written English becomes a status symbol, a marker for the ability to obtain private education and to travel abroad, and a sign of a cosmopolitan lifestyle.

The clash between Arabic and English has been heightened by the simultaneous decline in state funding for education and the rise in the percentage of Saudi students pursuing their studies in Saudi Arabia, the net result of which has been a decline in the competent use of English among the educated strata. With more and more Saudis obtaining higher education, the added demand for proficiency in English becomes a further hurdle to obtaining a good job in government or the professions. Those forced to remain in Saudi Arabia for their education thus feel doubly discriminated against. This attitude has been compounded by a growing resentment towards the expatriate labour force, most of whom use English as the language of communication. Young Saudis now see the demand for English literacy as a covert attempt to discriminate against them.

Asma (28), from Jeddah, studied accounting at King Abdul Aziz University in Jeddah but then realized she lacked English-language skills. To overcome this, she obtained her family's permission to spend the summer with relatives in London, where she successfully completed an English-language course. She then gained a Master's degree in business administration in Jeddah. Asma perceived the trip to London as necessary because of the deficiencies in the education system at home.

Dania (24), from Jeddah, speaks fluent English but claims she picked up the language on the street, during travels abroad with her family and from the Filipino maids at home. She also spoke English with her mother, who had studied it in Egypt. When I complimented her on her English-language skills, she commented that she had a 'decent standard of English'. For Dania, it was her affluent background and liberal family upbringing that provided her with the necessary exposure to learn English. Her identity as a member of the Saudi intelligentsia has been strengthened by her ability to communicate in English. Along with these skills comes a series of other symbols of cosmopolitan attitudes. For example, reading foreign-language books and newspapers gives her a window on the outside world that is denied to the majority of the population, and also allows her covertly to avoid the strictures of both religious and political censorship.

Adel (16) had the opportunity to study at the King Fahad Academy in London for one year. He is aware that proficiency in English is the route to success for his future career as a pilot based in Saudi Arabia. He says: 'I want to enrol at the King Faisal Flying Academy in Riyadh. After that, I want to become a pilot for Aramco because it is better than Saudia, the national airline.'

Likewise, Samir (15) had the chance to study English in London while his father was posted there. He is keen to become proficient in English in order to gain expertise in his future career as a mechanical engineer. Abdul Rahman says that English-language teaching remains a problem at the Saudi secondary school level, and in spite of his two years of study in the United States he still has difficulty with English classes at the university.

Ghalib (17), from Asir, continues to have serious difficulties with English despite the fact that he lives in London. This is probably 'because Saudis and other Arabs stick together throughout their stay in the host country'. He is keen to develop his language skills and hopes 'to enrol at King Fahad University in Dhahran, majoring in petroleum studies. I have a maternal uncle in the eastern province and my studies would always be linked in some way to my family.' In his opinion, 'there are many advantages in studying at a Saudi university, a main one being the availability of a wide variety of specializations'.

Sultan (15) says that 'the English language is an important asset because all jobs need languages'. His father wanted him to study law but his English is not strong enough, even after eight years in England, 'because the Arabs get together in London, and, even if they stay ten years, their English won't get better'.

Nader (16), from Mecca, has been living and studying at the King Fahad Academy in London since 1992. He wants to improve his English but is unsure of his future career. However, he says a degree from abroad will be more readily accepted as a passport to employment by Saudi companies. As for the education system, Nader says that it is not possible to fail an academic year in London as it would be in the Saudi system. In other words, Nader thinks the education system is much tougher in Saudi Arabia.

In a country where wealth and access to power bring increasingly visible advantages, the ability to speak fluent English has become yet another marker of privilege. It is flaunted to signify access and exposure to the West and the fruits of modern education and professionalism. The fact that two of the interviewees admitted they had failed to learn English when abroad because of their inability to mix further highlights this image. Worldly-wise, intelligent and mobile, Saudi Arabians who are proficient in English are esteemed while those who for social, economic or religious reasons fail to master the language are looked down upon as somehow involuntarily trapped in the Saudi Arabia of yesteryear.

The need to travel abroad

The social cachet attached to learning English is even greater when it comes to studying for university degrees abroad. Certainly the wealthy, the politically powerful and members of the royal family all opt to send at least their male children to universities in Europe and America. The United States is the prime destination of choice. Although American culture is demonized as *the* source of moral corruption in the world, the United States still retains the image of having the most advanced and sophisticated technology in the Western world. For many of the young people, experiencing the go-getting culture of America was one of its most attractive facets. Sami, for example, said that by studying in the United States he has become more 'aggressive' in seeking what he wants. Being separated from the relative certainties of home brought not only freedom from parental oversight but also freedom to compete in an environment alien to his own.

Mish'al, a member of the educated class, found that studying in America offered him the only way of obtaining an education in his chosen field of art. After completing his secondary education at the Capital Institute, one of Riyadh's top schools, he went to the United States for a university education. He acquired BA and MA degrees in art and graphic design and now wants to be a fashion designer. Mish'al pointed out that he could not have acquired this specialization had he stayed in Saudi Arabia. Furthermore, the country's censorship laws, which strictly comply with puritanical wahhabi Islam, would have prevented him from bringing his fashion magazines into the country as they are considered to represent indecent exposure of women. For Mish'al, the United States represented freedom from social as opposed to familial constraints. He also thinks it is the most advanced country in the West. As an entrepreneur who wants to set up his own fashion business he is aware of the competitive demands of the global economy. For him the United States is where he was going to 'learn the tricks from the masters'. Thus, the United States represented the pinnacle of capitalism that offered the best in his chosen subject as well as the freedom to develop his knowledge and personality in the way he wished.

Faiz, Amina and Abdul Rahman are representative of the majority of those interviewed whose parents could afford to send them abroad, and who commented that the advantages of education abroad were greater than those within the country.

For example, Faiz (16), from Ahsa, studied in Jeddah until the age of fifteen. His parents then sent him to one of the top private schools in the United States. When I asked him why he decided on an American education, he said it was better than a Saudi one 'because there are more facilities and a better environment to live in'.

Amina completed her secondary education in Jeddah, after which she was sent to a boarding school in England for two years. This, she explained, gave her the opportunity to acquire a better education than was available in Saudi Arabia, thereby preparing her for university. For her, unlike many others, learning English was not the main reason for going abroad, as she speaks English at home with her non-Saudi mother.

Abdul Rahman is studying at a university in the United States because he believes that the academic standards there will equip him with the necessary skills to deal with the realities of the outside world and to acquire a higher position at home. Like other young interviewees from wealthy families, he regards sending children abroad as a powerful symbol of status. Although not a rebellious act in itself, it can indicate a dissatisfaction with the status quo within Saudi Arabia. An American university, more than its Saudi counterpart, will satisfy the aspirations of wealthy Saudi parents, securing their status in an increasingly competitive society.

Malak (17), from Jeddah, had a different reason for travelling abroad. She is in the last year of secondary education, focusing on *adabi,* the arts, at the *al-furdous* school. She feels she has to travel abroad to study the history of Islamic art – a subject central to Saudi culture and self-image – believing that there is more knowledge and greater expertise to be found outside the national educational system.

For those wealthy enough to travel or for those with liberal parents who will permit them to travel, leaving Saudi Arabia provides a means of escaping what some see as the shortcomings of both education and society at large. However, the mass of the new generation lacks this option. Young women may well be stopped from studying abroad for financial reasons, but also because of the fear that out of reach of direct control they may bring shame on their family. A large section of those interviewed shared the negative views about the teaching they received in Saudi Arabia, but those unable to travel lack the means to improve the education they receive. This leads to anger and despair for those without wealth or connections. The cousins Jamila, Asia, Amel and Ahlam come from the educated class but are not well-off by Saudi standards. They are all in higher education and have aspirations to study abroad but 'travel is difficult … we have to study at the local colleges as best we can. Our families do not allow us to study abroad because they are afraid for us.' During the interview the mother of Jamila and Asia interrupted, saying, 'Although they were enthusiastic to travel we needed someone to take care of them. Now they are doing very well.' Jamila wishes to study abroad for a Master's degree in jewellery design for semi-precious stones. Unfortunately, she says, she has not been given permission or funds by her family to travel and continue her studies.

Problems of the education system

As already noted, in the 1970s and 1980s the government expanded the number and size of universities partly to enable male Saudis to fill positions in the state industries and the bureaucracy. Free education, housing, food and books were provided by the government and, until recently, a job was also guaranteed. The government encouraged a conservative approach to teaching by giving the *'ulama* supervisory controls over education policy, even in the secular universities, and this resulted in a strong Islamic influence on the largely expanded university curricula. Not only did education tend to turn out people with conservative attitudes, but also the teaching of foreign cultures and beliefs was restricted and foreign students were excluded from the state schools.[3] The expatriate communities have their own schools, which Saudi nationals are not allowed to attend. While foreigners are segregated from Saudis at all levels of the educational system, there are exceptions in cases of Arabs and of Arabic-speaking Muslims. The segregation in the national education system that aims at preserving 'Saudi' identity has not been particularly criticized by the interviewees. In other words, in all their opinions of the education system, the youth did not express any desire to join the schools of the expatriate communities.

Although the provision of education was greatly expanded, it still represented the conservatism of a state legitimated by a specific type of Islamic culture. This approach has restricted (but certainly not halted) the impact of education on the development of new cultural and social attitudes. Said (27), for example, who comes from a tribal background and now lives in Tabuk, maintains many characteristics of his rural upbringing even while aspiring to an education for career reasons. He studied at King Abdul Aziz University in Jeddah, and, despite attending a school in Britain to acquire proficiency in English, for 'international business dealings', he cannot converse in English. Said actively cultivates his Arab and Islamic identity.

In contrast, Mish'al said that because of the influence of the media on his generation, particularly satellite television, 'if I were a schoolboy today I would despise what I was taught because of the conservatism and

---

[3] Cyril and Christine Simmons, 'Personal and Moral Adolescent Values in England and Saudi Arabia', *Journal of Moral Education*, Vol. 23, No. 1, 1994, pp. 3–15.

limited curriculum'.

This domination of higher education by the *'ulama* has led to a general rise in complaints by Saudi students about the curriculum's lack of relevance to their everyday practical needs. Rasha (27), from Mecca, thinks that university in Saudi Arabia has a 'bad' approach: 'Universities teach you what does not benefit you in the world.' When Rasha has children she plans to have them study in Saudi Arabia up to the age of fifteen or sixteen, then she will send them abroad unless a considerably different university curriculum is introduced in Saudi Arabia. Rasha argues that any reorganization of the educational system has to be undertaken with the right objectives. It must aim at 'making a distinction between religion and the achievements of society'.

Adnan (24), from Mecca, claims that at university in Jeddah all he studied was *nazariiya* (theory), based mainly on reading books. Asked whether this satisfied his career aspirations, he answered, 'Not at all; it was too basic.' Asked whether he thought any reforms needed to be introduced at the level of secondary school, he said his education before university had been mainly concerned with

> repetition at the *ibtida'i* (elementary) and then *i'dadi* (secondary) level. A totally new approach for schools at the *ibtida'i* level is needed. At the moment both secondary and elementary education concentrate on memorization rather than *fihm* (understanding). Also, the over-emphasis on religious education is at the expense of other subjects. Compared with universities abroad, some of the universities are good: King Fahad in Dahran, which is good in petroleum studies, while King Saud University is good for administrative studies. But change is not only a matter of spending more money; it must focus on *al-tanzeem* (the organization) of courses.

Adnan criticized the staffing policy of the main universities: 'The Egyptian staff are not good; some foreigners (such as the Americans) are good, but Saudis must be prepared to replace them at these universities.'

Many of those who have gone through the national educational system make a clear distinction between autonomous thought and learning by rote. Autonomous thought, they argue, should be nurtured by the system, but instead the ability to memorize large amounts of text is considered a sign of proficiency. Hadi (23), who completed his secondary education and one year of university in Riyadh, said reorganization of the national educational system was necessary 'to stop stuffing the brain. We treat a child as a child, but in the West a child is treated as a man. He is given respect from an early age to learn and think.' Abdul Hamid (23) who is being trained in the British system, develops this theme, asserting that 'foreign "Western" education teaches you how to think while Saudi education emphasizes learning by rote'.

Dania, a teacher, was asked how her education had prepared her for her career. She answered that although the Saudi university system was 'not bad, I myself worked and advanced on a private basis. I had to seek out good advice at the right time, in the right place. I always tell my students, "this is your only chance; make the most of it".' She strongly believes that education has a great influence on general attitudes and personality. Because of her education, she has learned to live a better life and to enhance its qualities. However, family background influenced her more than formal education. On the basis of her experience as a student and a teacher, she believes that 'the university curriculum does not compete with the realities of the Saudi world'. In order to succeed, those who cannot travel abroad have to work much harder.

Dania criticizes pre-university teaching. She believes that many changes ought to be introduced at the secondary school level, including abolishing all extra religious courses. In addition, she says that there is a great deal of repetition and unnecessary overlap between the intermediate and secondary levels of schooling:

> We have to respect intellectual questioning, that is, the ability to raise questions and be objective should always be upheld. The same problems run through the university system. Why do I have to teach students four levels of Islamic culture when they know nothing about Napoleon and the World Wars? Saudi universities teach our people how to be lazy and how to fool the system. People fit into strict rules.

In reply to a question about relying on foreign guidance in Saudi education, Dania said: 'Knowledge lies everywhere,' and that she does not distinguish between East and West, Islamic and other.

Malak (17) underlined the traditional practice of teaching when she said: 'In the schools teachers do not care if you understand as long as you memorize.' Although critical of the schools, Malak says she loves the *ihtiram* (respect for tradition) and regrets that there is less and less respect in society, blaming the decline on the values of modernity, which stress only material comforts. Yet for Malak, tradition is not the extremism of the religious authorities who impose religious values on others and restrict educational aspirations. 'In order to be part of the global community we need to become more international while keeping something for ourselves.' Sami (30), educated in computer science at the University of Jeddah and in the United States, says that his aspiration is not to make money but to be the 'best man' in his field. He believes that in the future life will be more difficult and that it is necessary to adapt to science and technology because these are the only means to develop the economy. He says that his education in the United States has made him more competitive, an attribute that is necessary for survival in the new conditions of the future.

What is apparent from the interviews is that the young are increasingly aware of the demands that the outside world will place on them as adults. With cutbacks in government spending, social welfare programmes are no longer assured. A new sense of competition is spreading through the younger generation, driven by increasing unemployment. This has made young people focus on the deficiencies of the educational system. What has developed is a dichotomous view of Saudi approaches to learning in comparison to the West. In Saudi Arabia independent thinking is discouraged, and students are restricted by being forced to memorize without analysis. At the same time, with increased exposure to the outside world, the new generation has become more aware that in education more than elsewhere the *'ulama* are imposing restrictions that could be potentially harmful. Although it seems unfair to blame the *'ulama* for all the shortcomings of the Saudi educational system, they are the most visible target for young people, who perceive that their education is not allowing them to interact on an equal basis with the rapidly changing wider world that they know exists beyond the borders of Saudi Arabia.

Conclusion

By opening its own universities in 1957, the state has attempted to reduce the potential for education to provide a source of destabilizing views. By placing its official interpretation of Islam at the core of junior and secondary education, the state has also sought to inculcate a conservative outlook in order to restrict the forces of 'Western' political, social and cultural ideas as well as, more recently, the forces of globalization.

However, as Gregory Gause has argued, it is through the general educational system that national networks of political mobilization develop. These cut across family and tribal ties and mobilize people who share a similar outlook or social position.[4] The creation of the new middle class is largely a result of the expansion in education rather than the employment of large sections of the population in the state bureaucracy. So although Saudi society remains strictly hierarchical, through education the government has inevitably created a potentially restive constituency. The hierarchical order is changing with new economic and educational developments, and it is clear that the new generation has identified the restrictive nature of its education as a key focal point of dissatisfaction.

In contrast to political mobilization and democracy, neither of which features overtly in the state educational curriculum, there is heavy emphasis on the growth of nationalism and countrywide loyalty. The impact of this is to undermine or at least question regional, tribal and clannish allegiances and ties, reducing them to the basic unit of the extended family. Thus education and development of the middle class have enabled the smaller family groupings to become autonomous of larger family units. The curriculum itself stresses the unity of the Saudi nation. For example, considerable time and effort have been spent on homogenizing the national language. This was a gradual process whereby the distinctive Hijazi and Asiri dialects merged with the Nejdi and Ahsa dialects, thus producing a new Saudi version of Arabic spoken by the young and encouraged in schools. This distinguishes the new generation's speech from the dialects spoken by their grandparents. Regionalism has been marginalized within the official discourse. Furthermore, history and geography school textbooks emphasize Saudi Arabia's heroic national

[4] Gregory F. Gause, *Oil Monarchies: Domestic and Security Challenges in the Arab Gulf States.*

past and its unified territory. Likewise, religious books avoid the heterogeneous aspect of Islamic schools of thought and focus only on the *hanbali* version, and more specifically on its wahhabi interpretation. Thus, while on the one hand young people within the education system are showing frustration at the narrow, conservative basis of the curriculum, on the other hand they are gaining a sense of stability and coherence from its reliance on what is perceived as tradition, Islam and their nation, Saudi Arabia.

Education has led to the creation of the new middle class on the one hand, but on the other it continues to strengthen or reinforce the wealthy elite who have access to the best private schools in Saudi Arabia and are also able to send their children, especially sons, abroad for higher education. In these cases, children of the elite families receive foreign degrees and acquire proficiency in English, which ensures them the best jobs. In the present economic circumstances education, as a criterion of status, is beginning to assume a greater relative importance. In a situation of continuous social mobility based on non-economic factors, it assumes the most important non-economic role in terms of social competition. The circles of competition will become wider as women join the professions. Education and professional attainment will enhance the status of the elites, which had previously depended largely on social contacts, possession of wealth and good fortune.[5]

In the context of a society that has undergone rapid modernization over the past generation, family and education represent radically different influences. Among the older generation, the unquestioning upholding of 'traditional' attitudes and social values persists, and parents often try to transmit these to their children.

Despite the attachment to certain symbols of tradition, such as the veiling of women, traditional norms of respect for authority are changing. The new generation, which has been exposed to much more than its parents through education, satellite television and travel, is aware of its capabilities, and this inevitably leads to the questioning of some norms and social rules. This is by no means always overtly expressed because the fear of the unknown compels young people to turn back to a sense of security.

The result is a duality or conflict in cultural orientation, often repre-

---

[5] See Yamani, 'Formality and Propriety in the Hijaz'.

sented by relative proficiency in English. Mordechai Abir has noted the dilemma by citing the observation of a professor in the Saudi university system: 'English and Arabic are forces with powerful symbolic valence in Saudi Arabia; they stand for modern/traditional; secular/sacred; alien/comfortable.'[6] The dilemma is also represented by a conflict between modern and conservative teaching methods.

The younger generation is definitely conscious of the world beyond the borders of Saudi Arabia and believes that this is an arena where life possibilities would be enhanced. This is the normal perception even among young girls who have been sheltered from outside influences at home. Although there are both implicit and explicit frustrations with the quality of education, as well as with the existing censorship, there is also a sense in which the youth continue to cling to the family and the conventions of Saudi society as part of their social identity, and this will undoubtedly influence their future opinions about both political and cultural issues.

---

[6] Mordechai Abir, *Saudi Arabia in the Oil Era: Regime and Elites, Conflict and Collaboration* (London: Croom Helm, 1988), p. 170.

4 Ambitions and occupations in the contracting economy

The new generation of Saudi Arabia is in a unique and unenviable position. Its grandparents were the first to witness the emergence and expansion of a Saudi national economy, which broadened their horizons and raised their living standards. The pace of change quickened with the parents' generation, the first Saudis to interact with the world on the basis of an increasingly solid sense of national identity. The potentially disorienting speed of economic change was mediated through a stable and, for the most part, paternal state. The majority of Saudi Arabians of the parents' generation looked to the state to provide certainty; this meant that the state underwrote the financial stability of Saudi citizens. The state's role expanded beyond the provision of health care and education, to the direct employment of large sections of the male population, thus ensuring that a certain level of affluence was guaranteed across the country.

By contrast, the new generation is now beginning to recognize that state-guaranteed economic certainty is a luxury it can no longer depend on. The progressive decline in oil revenues in real terms has forced the Saudi government to scale back its spending on welfare provision. As ever increasing numbers of the new generation prepare to enter the job market they face the prospect of under-employment or even unemployment. The vast majority of those interviewed showed their awareness of this and were realistic about the state of the economy. They understand that the oil-driven economic boom has ended and that they themselves must take greater responsibility for their livelihoods.

Beyond the widespread acknowledgment of economic realities, however, the new generation is divided over what to do about it. On the basis of their approaches to the issues concerned it is possible to group the young Saudis interviewed into two broad categories: 'activists' and 'fatalists'. The activists are so called here because they have more of a 'can-do' attitude. They show that they have sought to identify the sources of Saudi economic weakness and to formulate ways of dealing with it, at both the collective or societal and the personal levels. In diagnosing society's ills and suggesting remedies, the 'activists' divide into two groups. The first group espouses liberal ideas demanding transparency and accountability of the government and blaming the corruption and inefficiency of the ruling elite for the problems. Broadly reformist in approach, this group would want to institute greater fairness in wealth distribution by the state, making governmental largesse open to all according to need and skill and not family connection. At the personal level the liberal activists tend to focus on individual improvement along professional lines. Such young people, many educated abroad, identify in what they see as traditional Saudi attitudes a fatalism and lack of discipline that have caused the national economy to descend into inefficiency. Through the adoption of Western and specifically American management techniques they see themselves and their peers reorganizing business practices to face the challenge of the globalized economy.

By contrast, the second group of activists approaches problems at the societal level in a broadly Islamic way. These activists claim the economy is in decline because of the unchallenged corrupting influences of the West, and that the large-scale involvement of US companies and personnel in the Saudi economy is a symbol of Saudi impotence and therefore should be ended. This approach is highly moralistic in tone and sees the untrammelled influence of modernity on the economy as the enemy. It also identifies the ruling elite as corrupt and seeks to deploy Islam as a means of reforming the whole of society.

The second category, the 'fatalists', also divides into 'liberal' and religious. For these people, it is either the hand of Allah or a rejuvenated oil market that will set the Saudi Arabian economy back on the right track. Either way, they look to greater forces, the international economy, the Saudi state or the hand of God to secure their fate and determine their living standards. They fail to take any responsibility for the current economic problems, either personal or societal. They may blame the present government but do not wish to be involved in its reform. They certainly do not feel motivated towards greater personal autonomy or individual betterment to lessen their chances of experiencing radically reduced living standards.

71

Rasha (27), from Mecca, sums up the general pessimism one finds among the new generation: 'At the rate at which the Saudi economy is going down more Saudis will soon not be working. Saudi society will not become richer.' She broadly blames the ruling elite's approach to governing the Kingdom. 'The future depends on the economy, but the government cannot impose tax because the ruling family receive a salary, free travel and other expenses. This has to be eliminated before tax is imposed.' Like most of the new generation, she proposed a solution that is not revolutionary but meritocratic: 'The public sector should find things to do for the young generation. Government services are not equally accessible to all citizens and this should change.' While Rasha exemplifies the more liberal activist attitude, Arif (27), from Riyadh, is not worried about the changing economic circumstances because of his belief that 'Allah has provided Saudi Arabia with oil wealth and other blessings and will not fail His worshippers'. This belief is reflected in Arif's decision to have seven children despite the fact that his current family finances are fledgling. His philosophy here is that 'each child comes with its own *rizg* (provisions)'.

Economic decline

The Saudi economy started to decline in 1983 when oil prices dropped dramatically. This process accelerated after the 1990–91 Gulf War when the Kingdom had to find extra resources to pay for the costs incurred. Compared with the late 1970s and early 1980s, when Saudi foreign assets were at their highest, the Kingdom's overseas investments were greatly reduced. This prompted the government to take the unprecedented step of raising a loan from overseas banks in an attempt to avert a fiscal crisis. By early 1998, the economic situation was even more precarious, with the price of Saudi crude as low as 11 dollars per barrel. This necessitated a government policy of cutbacks and a reduced social security programme, as well as seeking international efforts to bring the prices back up.

According to the IMF, living standards in Saudi Arabia slipped from among the world's highest in 1981 to the level of a middle-income nation in 1993.[1] Individuals may still be rich, but as a society Saudi Arabia is

[1] *The Financial Times*, 22 December 1993.

not, and since the Saudi government can no longer afford high levels of expenditure on social services such as health and education it cannot maintain the role on which it was founded. Welfare and development have been the central tenets of the ruling ideology and have historically cushioned the indigenous population from the sort of social and political problems that are endemic in other Middle East and North African states.

The IMF has forecast increasing levels of indebtedness for Saudi Arabia, and has recommended further readjustment of development policies to reflect more accurately the market values of international finance.[2] The Kingdom derives around 75 per cent of government revenues from the oil sector, and public purchasing power has fallen in tandem with the fall in the real price of oil. 1993 registered slow growth of just one per cent, a balance-of-payments deficit of $19.4 billion on current account spending and a budget deficit averaging 11 per cent of GDP. By 1994 growth in GDP had fallen to 0.6 per cent, which represents a drop of 2 per cent in real terms. The government budget, in deficit since 1983, has mainly been funded by domestic borrowing, which is now becoming scarce.

Across-the-board budget cuts have been instituted – for example, a 20 per cent reduction in education spending in 1994 alone. From January 1995, Saudi Arabia was obliged to raise the cost of petrol, water, electricity and telephone rates. In 1997 the Ministry of Health proposed to charge patients at government hospitals in order to cut state expenditure.[3] The government needs to raise immense sums – about £81 billion for electricity alone – to keep infrastructure up to the mark and to encourage the return of the £375 billion-plus that Saudis hold abroad.[4] Furthermore, Saudi Aramco, the state oil company, has reached the end of a long period of capacity expansion. These measures are collectively hitting the Saudi public hard. The rising spectre of unemployment (unheard of until recently) and increasing reports of a crime wave have forced the government to initiate limited political reform and will throw all areas of government spending open to public debate.

---

[2] See, for example, Catherine Caufield, *Masters of Illusion: The World Bank and the Poverty of Nations* (Basingstoke: Macmillan, 1997).
[3] *Saudi Gazette*, 13 December 1997.
[4] David Hirst, *The Guardian*, 12 August 1999.

The state is the largest employer: an estimated 88 per cent of the workforce is in the public sector.[5] An IMF study of Saudi society in the 1970s showed that most Saudis with an education desired a government job because this was the most secure base from which to develop family life. Access to government influence, usually by family connection, is a common method of career advancement, resulting in a high degree of personal dependence by the individual on the state. The ruling family dominates this sector by employment contracts and control of positions in the bureaucracy and state utilities.

There is an assumption among some Western analysts that by accentuating Islamic values in education, especially the segregation of the sexes, the government has not prepared the population for the necessary structural adjustments that the economy and society will have to undergo in the coming decades. This analysis is apparent in World Bank reports as well as in the journals and newspapers that rely on them. However, this type of analysis offers little insight into how the economic and social restructuring of Saudi Arabia is affecting the lives and outlook of its population.

A large proportion of those interviewed for this study showed a keen awareness not only of the state of the economy but also of the sacrifices that would be imposed on their generation because of it. Abdul Muhsin (26), for example, said that 'in the past everything was easier. There were more opportunities.' He went on to acknowledge that 'this generation's living standards will not get better. The oil benefited my generation superficially. We got toys out of it while the older generation benefited most.' He highlighted the increasing intergenerational tension this reduction in living standards has caused. 'We are always discussing the economy with older cousins and brothers. They tell us that we are spoiled. This cannot be true because during the 1970s 30 to 40 per cent of the older generation had the chance to go abroad and find the right job. Their life was secure, highly admired and they were compensated. The smallest thing they did was considered impressive.' Abdul Wahid's views also highlight an increased polarization of Saudi society around access to wealth and power: 'The change in living standards between the generations is

---

[5] Bob Robinson, *The Saudi Labour Market: The Experience and Understanding of Saudi Development and Training Company* (Dammam: Saudi Development and Training Company Limited, Dammam, July 1996), p. 5.

relative to social class. Today the upper class have the same chances while the middle to lower class have more competition facing them.'

Abdul Wahid's views found echoes across the social and regional spectrum of those interviewed. Faiz (16), from Ahsa, also thinks the lives of his generation are going to be tougher: 'The future is going to be more competitive and it will not necessarily be easy to succeed. There will be more people with better education and all the business has already been done.'

Dania (24) was even more pessimistic. 'I do not think that anybody will maintain the living standards of their parents' generation. The times of the *tafra* (boom) are over; they have to close the palaces and send away most of the servants.' Suhair (27), from Najran, confirms this view when she says that the living standards of the previous generation could not possibly be re-created. 'They [our parents] have *'azayim* (feasts) for hundreds of people, but they also have *ba'zagha* (waste) of a hundred things.'

Youssef (15), from Ras Tannoura, believes the problem is the economy's dependence on petrochemicals. 'Oil', he says, 'will be a dead end. It will run out in forty years, therefore we must turn our country into one less dependent on oil.' Saudi Arabia is the foremost example of a GCC state that has undergone major societal transformation in a relatively short period of time. It is certainly not a coincidence that Saudi Arabia has also recently witnessed demands for political and social reform in the face of uncertainty.

Fiscal austerity poses an immediate problem: how to accommodate the growing numbers of the new generation reaching the job market. The rapid population growth that accompanied the modernization of Saudi society creates a unique problem for the integration of this generation into society. The public sector is already over-manned and the potential of the private sector to employ Saudi nationals has been impeded by a variety of cultural and economic factors.

With young people representing such a large percentage of the population, the state's inability to provide them with employment will in the long term prove a major source of social tension that could result in the destabilization of the current regime. Yassir (22), who was educated in Riyadh, realizes his prospects are greatly reduced in comparison with previous generations. 'Unemployment', he observed, 'is a big problem'. Yassir believes that there is no hope that Saudi society will become richer.

'Things are going in a direction with no good omens. Wealth is decreasing and will continue to do so and we are allowed to have no opinion on this subject.'

Employers in the private sector must operate in a global market and, as a result, prefer not to engage in the costly job-training programmes promoted by the government for nationals. The Council of Saudi Chambers of Commerce and Industry has attempted to circumvent private-sector resistance to retraining. It has spearheaded an initiative to set up training programmes and thus aid Saudi-ization. The government has been trying to encourage private firms to take on and train Saudi nationals for several years. For example, the Ministry of Labour and Social Affairs demanded in 1998 that all personnel advertisements in newspapers should emphasize that vacancies were for Saudi nationals only.[6]

The spectre of Saudi unemployment

As indicated in the Preface, it is difficult to get an accurate idea of the scale of the unemployment problem in Saudi Arabia, as population figures are riven with inconsistencies and vary considerably from one source to another. Of the estimated workforce of 5.7 million in 1990 (including nationals and expatriates), 624,800 (10.8 per cent) were said to be employed in the government sector; for Saudi nationals, as indicated above, the proportion was 88 per cent.[7] Saudi nationals working in the private sector are generally self-employed, business owners or managers; very few work in manual trades.

Although there are Saudi women in the workforce, the percentage is significantly lower than that of men – some commentators put the figure at no more than 5.5 per cent of working-age Saudi women. According to 1994 population estimates, the total number of men in the working age group (20–60 years) is close to 5,947,000. Including only those 270,000 or so Saudi females employed in the Kingdom and ignoring other Saudi women, the total labour pool (Saudis and expatriates) was about 6,200,000 in 1994.

[6] See the *Saudi Gazette*, 23 September 1998.
[7] Robinson, *The Saudi Labour Market*, p. 5.

Since expatriate males are, almost by definition, in employment, it is clear that there must have been significant unemployment among Saudis, assuming the figures are reliable. The only other explanation would be that over one million jobs were created for Saudis between 1990 and 1994, which seems much too high. The government has conceded that there are some 100,000 unemployed. But the Ministry of Social Affairs blamed Saudi businesses for the figure. In December 1997 he claimed that the problem was due to their employment practices. Independent estimates of unemployment vary, with analysts putting the figure at between 10 and 20 per cent of the domestic workforce. Other sources state that the unemployment rate is 27 per cent for native males and 95 per cent for females, with the added peculiarity that some six million expatriates toil on behalf of the 16 million Saudis.[8] Surveys by the Saudi Development and Training Co. indicate that the total number of expatriates in the 1990 labour force was 2,878,000, 60 per cent of the total labour force. In 1995, for example, Jeddah's workforce was estimated at 600,000, of which 500,000 were expatriate labour. These percentages are not expected to change before the year 2005. In the cities, where 78.5 per cent of the total Saudi population live, this situation has become a particular cause of social tension in recent years. This is especially true of the younger generation of Saudis, who must compete with foreigners when seeking employment. Saudis do take up positions in the more desirable banking sector, where they comprise 65–70 per cent of the workforce, as well as in the privately owned petrochemical industries, where more than 50 per cent of the migrant workers are unskilled.

The basic law of government decrees that the state shall provide job opportunities to all able-bodied people. Unemployment causes problems for many young people, as Hamad (29), from the southern tribes of Asir, laments:

The unemployment situation upsets us. I am now unemployed. We are struggling. My brother's salaries are two thousand riyals each per month in a very expensive country. If it wasn't for my father, who has one of my brothers with his wife and children living with him in a flat, my brother would have been unable to cope with the rent. Likewise my

---

[8] David Hirst, *The Guardian*, 11 August 1999.

maternal and paternal cousins help those who are unemployed in the family. We all help each other materially because the economic situation is tiring. If the extended family does not embrace each other, human beings cannot survive because the state does not help you.

Government and the economy

Although the new generation is united in recognizing the problem of economic decline there are competing views about the sources of the problem and how to tackle it. The policy option of raising revenue by direct taxation of the indigenous population has brought to the surface previously latent criticisms of the government. Now that economic resources are perceived to be increasingly scarce their distribution has become a key issue. Although there is no organized movement demanding equality of distribution there are calls for greater transparency in economic decision-making. The new generation wants the system to be much more equitable, especially on the issue of welfare provision, and there is anger that patronage and influence lead to large inequalities of distribution.

As members of the new generation are the first to be comfortable with a national identity, so they have a greater determination to be treated as autonomous citizens and not just grateful subjects. They see the problem of inefficiency as soluble and they want access to decision-making power to aid solutions. Their views can be summed up thus: 'We, the new generation, are the nation, but there are restraints upon us. We want to exercise more responsibility but cannot.'

There was a general recognition among all the interviewees that the distribution of state welfare provision was a problem. For those marginalized or with no access to patronage this gave rise to a strong sense of resentment and alienation from the state. Faiz is a young member of an important business family. A student of sixteen who has studied in Jeddah and the United States, he is clearly not disadvantaged or suffering because of the economic situation, but he still feels constrained within Saudi society. Strict social rules should be abolished, he says, because 'everything is permitted by Islam'. His second major point concerns equity. For Faiz, laws should be applied consistently. He complains that although satellite television in Saudi Arabia is illegal, 'the King had the biggest satellite [dish] of all'. Interestingly, his argument is directed not against Western influence but at the contradictions that are thrown up by the authorities' apparent inability to modify the way they rule in these times of change. Sami picks up on the theme of corruption and the abuse of power. He sees the problems in society in stark terms since returning from the United States. 'We have no basic necessities. We cannot get mobile phones unless we have *wasta*. If the water is cut off from your home it cannot be fixed without *wasta*. Things that you take for granted abroad we do not have here so the average person suffers.' He thinks that the problem is the nature of the government 'that controls everything'; instead, he argues, 'we need to develop the private sector'.

The majority of those among the new generation who have formulated a coherent critique of the state focus on the use of *wasta* or influence to gain preferential treatment. Fahad (23) develops this theme by saying: 'Everyone knows there are complaints about the welfare system. Poor people do not get the government help they need. This results in the rich becoming more rich and the poor becoming more poor.' Fahad says that government services are not equally accessible to all Saudis. He complains that there are people who receive a salary without working. Furthermore, 'everything requires *wasta*. There are those who receive VIP treatment without deserving it. At the *takhasusi* (specialist government hospital) the rich do not pay, taking the benefits from the poor. The government employment services should be more correct.'

These young people (even those who are privileged) clearly regard the way the state functions with respect to the distribution of wealth in relation to their career development as unacceptable. There is an increasing concern that the government is failing to help those most in need. Again the demands are reformist as opposed to revolutionary in nature; very few of the new generation are calling for the removal of the government or even a change in personnel. They want efficiency to be facilitated by equality.

One of the issues of economic policy that divides the new generation is whether the government can and should impose direct taxation on the population. Again this raises key issues of equity and efficiency. Adnan (24) thinks that Saudi Arabia 'is getting poorer and poorer'. He is also critical of King Fahd. 'The King, *allah yahfazu* (God keep him), is not helping us at all and is in fact making things worse.' But he thinks there is no need for taxes, since they are already being imposed on the people indirectly, and that much of the existing pricing system actually incorporates many such indirect taxes. Fahad agrees with him on this point. Although he does not believe that Saudi society will become richer he still thinks direct taxes are a bad idea: 'More than this!', he exclaimed. He says that indirect taxes have been combined with budget cuts. 'They already impose cuts, for example from petrol [subsidies] which has become expensive for us.'

When I asked Abdul Rahman (18), from Riyadh, about the possible decline of the living standards of the new generation relative to that of its parents, he made a strong point about government probity. Before anything could be done, he argued, 'we first want to know what our assets are. We are not clearly told by our governments what we have and what we do not.' Samir (15), from Riyadh, agrees, for although 'Saudi Arabia remains a rich country with a wealthy stratum, the poor need help'. The problem is that 'there is disparity of wealth'. He adds: 'We are behind and very much dependent on oil. We should not rely on oil nor on the Americans.'

The perceived dependence on the United States is a common theme. Increasingly the American link is seen as both restrictive and emasculating. Among the more conservative of the new generation it is this which is to blame for all Saudi Arabia's problems. Said (27) comes from the north of the country. He condemns the luxuries of consumer society and sees it as the work of the Americans, who, in his view, want to keep the Saudis dependent upon them. He blames the government for this dependency: 'It is the government that spoiled people who cannot be out in the sun any more since they have experienced the comforts of air-conditioning. The government created the *ittikali* (rentier mentality).' Said's views are representative of a large minority of the new generation and suggest the continuing popularity of conservative values among the young, who reject developments they see as eroding Arab and Islamic virtues. For Said, it is television that has made the new generation into consumers of material culture. He thinks that the United States is behind the whole thing because 'they want us to remain dependent upon them'. So the external threat of the United States representing the evil of modernization is the driving force behind the emasculation of Saudi society. But Said places the blame for this on the government: they should (and still could) resist this influx of an alien culture and values.

Employment, the Saudi-ization of the workforce and foreign workers

To be a Saudi has in the past meant to be assured of a job, but not just any job. Employment must be representative of social status so white-collar jobs that indicate education and responsibility have a high social cachet. Even with increasing economic uncertainty there are clearly jobs that young Saudis cannot imagine doing. For example, Sahar (30), from Jeddah, cannot see any way to substitute Saudi Arabians for the large numbers of foreign domestic helpers. This is because of the stigma attached to doing domestic work for other families. She comments: 'Even if a Saudi woman was starving, she would not work for anyone else.' Nader (16), from Mecca, says that 'we do not need so many foreigners working in Saudi Arabia'; however, 'we do need the Indians to do the menial work. These are jobs difficult for the Saudis to do.'

Most of the young people interviewed prefer to maintain a social distance from the foreigners employed in Saudi Arabia. Saad (16), from the eastern province, commented that 'Saudis should keep a distance between themselves and expatriate workers. Their presence is a paradox because it causes unemployment.' Although segregation between Saudis and foreigners is not a new phenomenon, the latter's presence is increasingly questioned and causes resentment sometimes bordering on outright xenophobia.

During the 1970s as much as half the population of Saudi Arabia was made up of expatriate labour, drawn to the Kingdom during the oil boom to take part in the development and construction of the massive state-funded infrastructure projects. That was fine until demography dictated a rising indigenous demand for employment. It is this that has fuelled resentment towards non-Saudi labour. Saudis feel they are in direct competition with foreign workers, especially those who are better qualified and have stronger language skills.

Currently, Saudi Arabians make up only 4 per cent of the personnel in the non-oil industrial sector of the economy, with a mere 12 per cent in the service sector.[9] Between 1994 and 1996, figures show a 5 per cent annual growth in the number of foreign workers. These non-Saudis are either more qualified or more likely to accept jobs that are refused by Saudis, as well as more likely to receive much lower wages than their Saudi counterparts.[10] For example, a survey by the Higher Commission for Riyadh Development found that 16 per cent of Saudis employed in the city were in skilled jobs. The vast majority (81 per cent) were employed in either managerial, professional or supervisory roles.[11]

The foreign workers are not merely in blue-collar occupations; they are engineers, doctors, academics and technicians whose work is essential for the functioning of all sectors of the economy. Thus replacing them requires not only an enormous structural and policy change on the part of the government, but also a shift in certain attitudes of the new generation before they reach the job market.

As a response to the growing numbers of graduates entering the job market, the Saudi government initiated protective labour regulations, so-called Saudi-ization policies. The Fifth Development Plan (1990–95) and the Sixth Development Plan (1996–2001) envisaged that the way out of the dilemma was to reduce the number of non-Saudis in the labour force and replace them with Saudis. The plans suggested an increase in Saudi employment by 4.2 per cent annually, while reducing the rate of expatriate employment by 1.2 per cent annually.[12] The Saudi-ization programmes of the Fifth Development Plan did not anticipate an increase in the non-Saudi workforce. On the contrary, their number was expected to go down as Saudi nationals replaced them. The stated aim of the sixth five-year plan (1995–2000) was to 'replace non-Saudis with appropriately qualified and willing-to-work Saudi manpower in all occupations' and to develop 'Saudi manpower through meticulous evaluation of educational curricula and training programmes'.[13]

This resulted in a series of legislative initiatives. The Sixth Development Plan aimed to create 659,000 new jobs by 2000, 50 per cent of these through Saudis replacing foreign workers. The government stipulated

[9] *The Financial Times*, 20 December 1995.
[10] Mohammad Abdallah Al-Ghayth and Mansour Abdul-Aziz Al-Ma'shouq, 'National Employment in the Saudi Private Sector', *Public Administration*, No. 82, March 1994, pp. 125–57 (in Arabic).
[11] Figures quoted in the Economist Intelligence Unit, *Saudi Arabia Country Report*, 1st quarter, 1998.
[12] Saudi Ministry of Planning, *Fifth Development Plan: 1990–1995*, p. 119.
[13] 'Saudi Arabia', *MEED Special Report*, Vol. 39, No. 10, 10 March 1995, p. 40.

that companies with twenty or more employees had to increase their number of Saudi employees by 5 per cent per annum or else forfeit government loans and contracts. Unfortunately, the result was to impede business expansion and even to encourage the fragmentation of businesses into smaller units, at a time when Saudi business advisers were suggesting that family companies should incorporate to expand business operations hampered by family management practices.

The government has also specified 26 professions that are to be closed to non-Saudi nationals. At the end of 1997, it stipulated that all administrative staff and 50 per cent of drivers working for transport companies must be Saudi nationals. It has also increased the cost of foreign labour by raising the cost of social security and work permits. In a more indirect attempt to discourage foreign labour, the Ministry of Commerce has instructed companies to issue all their domestic correspondence in Arabic, challenging the predominant use of English.

This strategy had the negative effect of increasing the use of un-registered workers. To stem this trend, the government also began to target the large numbers of Hajj pilgrims who stay behind to work as domestic helpers in Saudi homes. As part of this drive it expelled 500,000 illegal workers in October and November 1997.[14]

The structural effects of the government's Saudi-ization plan are of little interest to the vast majority of the new generation. But they are well aware that to date it has not been a success. Again, explanations for this tend to focus on external sources of blame. Majid, for example, states that:

> the Saudi-ization programme is not very successful because of politics. When I was working in the refinery company they disposed of a few foreigners, but because they were Westerners, they redirected them to another refinery company, despite the fact that it was acknowledged they were not as qualified as the Saudis. This is to do with political relations between our government and theirs and the Saudi citizens get left out.

The search among the new generation for an external source to blame for economic decline and cultural change is common. As economic conditions have visibly declined young people have been plagued by insecurity and

[14] The Economist Intelligence Unit, *Saudi Arabia Country Report,* 1st quarter, 1998.

uncertainty, and they have selected various groups to bear responsibility. As criticizing the government and the ruling elite is potentially very dangerous, new, easier targets have been found. Rising tension owing to the presence of large numbers of foreign workers has thus become very noticeable.

This foreign presence is especially troubling because on one level it threatens unemployment and on another it highlights deficiencies in the Saudi labour market. Why has the country become so dependent upon itinerant labour so obviously alien to the indigenous population, especially when there has been no process of homogenization through schooling or social practices? For the new generation the answer to this question is not easy. Samir, for example, accepts the large number of South Asian workers in the Kingdom but becomes troubled when talking about the Americans he sees as dominating management posts: 'Are they more intelligent than us?', he asks. 'This is the insult.'

On the one hand, many of those questioned see the presence of foreign labour as an indictment of Saudi attitudes to work. Why is there a need for other people to do the hard labour and menial tasks in this society? On the other hand, seeing the large number of Americans and Europeans in high-ranking jobs receiving higher pay wounds both personal and national pride. Young men interviewed complained about the salaries in most professional spheres; in hospitals an American doctor is paid more than the British and the British more than a Saudi. Saudis should be capable of making decisions and running their own economy. Either they can perform these tasks and are prevented from doing so or they cannot because they have not received the right training. Either way the inference is that the government and powerful Saudi businessmen are to blame.

A more immediate reaction is to see foreigners as the main cause of unemployment, to remove them and allow surplus Saudi labour to be deployed. In the opinion of Haifa (16), from Riyadh, 'the biggest achievement for Saudi Arabia would be to get rid of the foreigners and hence solve the unemployment problem. We give our money to the foreigners.' But different groups of foreigners are seen variously as the bringers of much-needed skills or the carriers of moral corruption. Those who are more activist in their perspective may simultaneously resent Americans while accepting the South Asian workers as a necessary evil.

Haifa asserts: 'Petrol has been the means by which the Americans manipulated us. Saudi Arabia gave America too much, more than it should have taken.' Amani (15) agrees; she thinks that there are too many foreigners in the country and that 'we allow the Americans to control everything. Saudi Arabians should be given priority in the job market. The problem is that we believe that the foreigner has more experience. Thus we have fewer Saudis in the workforce.'

The opinions expressed above show that in terms of identity formation, the rising economic uncertainty has led the new generation increasingly to definine themselves as Saudi Arabians in a negative sense. They juxtapose themselves against the large numbers of foreigners in their midst. They employ South Asians because they 'cannot possibly' do domestic, menial or labouring jobs themselves. But the Americans and Europeans pose a bigger problem of definition. It is easier to blame this class of expatriate labour for fostering Saudi dependency on them. The Americans must be present in such numbers because of some underhand plot! How come Saudi businesses prefer to employ foreign workers? Mish'al (29), from Riyadh, gives his reason. Having returned home after studying fashion and design in the United States, he is now trying to set up a clothes factory. He says he would employ Egyptian, Indian and Filipino workers because of their expertise in this industry, and 'the Saudis do not want to work'. Sami (30), from Jeddah, disagrees, arguing that Filipinos, for example, do not necessarily perform better than Saudis. For him it is a matter of cost. Saudis are discriminated against because they cannot work for the same low wages as Asian expatriates.

So the younger generation is now forced into a job market where secure government jobs have become scarce and where employers have a preference for foreign workers. Young people believe they see uncaring employers supported by devious foreigners intent upon protecting themselves by creating barriers to indigenous applicants. They believe they know a double standard when they see one. Adnan (24) argued that 'most Saudi business corporations actually make it much more difficult for Saudis to apply because of very strict conditions. The end result is that only foreigners would get the job, especially since they cost less to hire.' He went on to say that the presence of an expatriate community posed problems: 'Some expatriates commit crimes, especially those who are unemployed and are sitting on the streets.' In terms of local universities, 'the Egyptian staff are not good; some foreigners like the Americans are good, but Saudis must be prepared to replace them at these universities'.

With the general use of English as a discriminator in achieving employment and a generally limited capability in terms of job search and self-marketing, Saudi youth are increasingly finding the employment search a degrading and frustrating experience.[15]

For the new generation the lack of employment opportunities is the key factor fuelling their sense of insecurity and self-doubt. The visible presence of large numbers of non-Saudis throughout the economy highlights their feeling that something is wrong with their society. The presence of Americans and Europeans in responsible and prestigious jobs leads them not only to question their own skills but also to look askance at the employers who hire these people over themselves. It is all too easy to resort to racism and to conspiracy theories to explain away these difficult questions. Attitudes towards the expatriates differ according to the social and religious inclinations of the youth: the more conservative and religious activists make a distinction between Muslims and non-Muslims and believe the former should be tolerated not only on grounds of necessity but also for religious reasons. Meanwhile, those with relatively more liberal ideas make a distinction based on professional efficiency or need. On the whole ethnic tensions prevail, especially *vis-à-vis* the Pakistanis and Indians. Hamad sums up this latent racism: 'When we were little we used to throw tomatoes at them [the Indians]. We were small kids being foolish, but the adults watching us walked along and said nothing.' Hamad, like others, knows that racism is illegal under Islamic law, on which the Saudi constitution is based. The Quran itself provides guidance on this matter. At the most general level it is broadly permissive of potential marriage partners. It states: 'O mankind! We have created you from a single [pair] of a male and a female, and made you into nations and tribes, that ye may know each other. Verily the most honoured of you in the sight of Allah is the most pious of you.'[16] But members of the new generation are increasingly being forced to question the cultural attitudes that mean they will not perform manual jobs. They are also questioning the education system that apparently leaves them unprepared to replace expatriate workers in high-powered jobs.

[15] Bob Robinson, *The Saudi Labour Market*, pp. 14–18.
[16] Quran, *Surat* 49, *al-Hujurat* (The Inner Apartments), no. 49, verse 13.

Patronage and Saudi management style

Employment and career advancement through access to influence within government has now become a major issue of discussion among the new generation. A growing resentment at fellow Saudis' approach to management is especially detectable in those educated abroad. The dominance of family relations in the workplace is often cited as a major problem. Kinship and the family still dominate social and economic relations, to the extent that a government minister, once appointed, will employ large numbers of his relatives within the ministry administration. The family structure of private business very often makes it difficult for non-family members to break in. The reaction to this by the new generation is twofold. Some perceive this 'traditional' approach to business and the economy as anachronistic. Influenced by experiences from outside the kingdom they seek to implement more rational, efficient and depersonalized approaches to management. Others, while seeing 'traditional' approaches as normal, resent them nonetheless for excluding them from access to jobs. Both approaches call for reform of Saudi management styles, but for different ideological and practical reasons.

For their part, many employers claim that Saudi nationals are not adaptable to employment and business because of cultural attitudes that encourage regional and family preferences. Hence, Nejdis prefer to stay resident in the Nejd, Hijazis in the Hijaz, whereas expatriate communities are mobile and adaptable. Employers have attempted to encourage geographical mobility by employing young Saudis on what have become known as 'unmarried contracts'. It is believed that single males are more flexible and can be posted to different parts of the country.[17] Even so, most businesses in Saudi Arabia are family-owned, and because of this there is an unwillingness to allow any Saudi national from outside the family access to business information.

Although Mish'al (29) complains that the Saudis do not want to work, at the same time he likes the custom of *ihtiram* (respect) and says that the younger generation should not 'exceed their boundaries'. This is but one illustration of the ambivalence of young Saudis towards the sort of social changes that would be needed for effective economic restructuring. As

[17] See, for example, the *Saudi Gazette*, 20 May 1998.

we have seen, the new generation is placed within a society that provides it with an identity and has in the past been the main source of stability. But it realizes society has to be reformed to continue to meet the needs of the young. If this process of reform goes too far it will attack the very sense of certainty they are trying to preserve.

Other young men with exposure to American cultural values are also upset about the habits of Saudi employees and employers. Sami (30) contrasted the aggressiveness and efficiency of American business culture with the *inshallah*, *bukra* and *maleish* ('Allah willing', 'tomorrow' and 'it is all right') attitudes of Saudis to work. He said that finding a job in Saudi Arabia was very frustrating because of the employers' attitude of *maleish* and *haram aleikum*. *Haram aleikum* is an approach that protects those to whom employers feel either a personal obligation as friends or through family connections or else a moral obligation, such as that towards *abu 'iyal*, a man who needs a job because he has children to support. This has an impact upon business efficiency as well as labour mobility. Sami goes on to say that even the basic necessities require *wasta* in Saudi Arabia. At the same time, in his view peoples' expectations are limited because of the excessive dependency of society on the government, and he believes that government controls should be relaxed and the private sector developed.

The issue of *wasta* is a central complaint of those interviewed. Samir (15), from Riyadh, for example, says: 'The problems of finding a job in Saudi Arabia are many. A university graduate in agriculture could through *wasta* end up as a religious teacher. Anything could happen through *wasta*.' But this is not necessarily a negative thing for the new generation. Amina (18), from Jeddah, when asked how she will get a job, replies: 'Through contacts. Contacts will get you there. Using contacts is a Saudi trait.' For her, as for so many Saudi Arabians, patronage humanizes an otherwise cold and uncaring bureaucracy. The daunting and potentially undermining task of obtaining a job can be made personal by the use of family contacts. By deploying contacts she has effectively spread the burden of worry about her prospects such that were she to be rejected, it would become an issue for the whole family. But this attitude is clearly not universally accepted. Omar (16), for instance, complains: 'All this [access to jobs and wealth] depends on the class and tribe of the person.' He believes that there should be no tribalism: 'All Saudi

Arabians should unite.' Rasha agrees: 'In Saudi Arabia you are personally not in a position to do anything. People respect your opinion depending on who you are, not what you are, your tribal belonging, not your education or personal merit.'

Conclusion

Said highlights the tension of the new generation, which has to operate in a globalized economy but wants the certainties of a localized culture. He recognizes the need to develop skills and to make international contacts for his business, but otherwise he shows a strong attachment to the ancestral home where his father has recreated a farm reminiscent of the pastoral days. In spite of widespread travel and higher education in business administration, Said still remains insular in his attitudes. His aspirations are limited to working in the family business with his brothers. When in the United Kingdom, he spent most of his time in Saudi upper-class circles because he says he was eager to make connections with important patrons. But by spending most of his time in London mixing with his compatriots he failed to master English, the reason for his stay. By only mixing with Saudis he insulated himself from a challenging and potentially disorienting environment.

For Said, as for the new generation as a whole, the situation is unprecedented and challenging. The paternal and ever-present state that supplied certainty to their parents has been forced to scale back its support, and this has made the lives of Saudi young people increasingly uncertain. When they search for explanations and solutions for the problems they face, even more contradictions are thrown up. When looking abroad, especially to the United States, for inspiration they find that the very state that has in the past underwritten their certainty may now be part of the problem. These problems have driven the almost universal pessimism that I found when interviewing. The new generation clearly understands that its standards of living are not going to improve in the foreseeable future. This pessimism has given rise to a resentment that increasingly attaches itself to the foreign workers in the Kingdom. The national identity of the young people is being framed by a negative hostility to those whom they see as taking their jobs. In the short term this means that social unrest may be directed away from the government, but in the long run this may turn into a disturbing trend that could further undermine attempts to restructure the Saudi economy.

Apart from this hostility to outsiders, the new generation's search for solutions remains unfocused. It seems to have polarized around two ideas. The first, more common among the 'fatalists' and the conservative Islamists, carries political ramifications since it pins the blame on external forces. It is America or the West or modernity that is to blame. If these malign influences can be reduced, Saudi Arabia can be strong and confident again. The second source of problems is more difficult for the young, for it focuses on their own state and society. This attitude is characteristic of the 'activists', both liberals and religious conservatives. Increasingly the government and the elite's style of rule are coming under sustained criticism. This is by no means a coherent or particularly radical assault. But the general sense of pessimism and unease has begun to see the government as the source of the problems faced by the country. Problems with Saudi society itself are even more difficult to understand, for by their very nature they involve some degree of self-censorship. There are the beginnings of an understanding that life cannot go on as it is in Saudi Arabia. The majority of the new generation, especially these 'activists', realize that ultimately they themselves must change if the future prospects are to improve.

5 Redefining patriarchy and gender identity

In Saudi Arabia today, as a result of educational and economic changes, demographic factors as well as wider cultural exposure, female members of the new generation express increasing frustration at the constraints that a patriarchally dominated society places on their life choices. However, the continuing centrality of Islam to their lives leads these young women to believe that change in their social status can only be achieved from within a religious frame of reference. The fact that this challenge to prevailing social norms has its foundations within an Islamic discourse means it has a resonance for large numbers of Saudi women irrespective of their social background. It also means that the demands for greater equality made with reference to Islam garner legitimacy within wider Saudi society.

Interestingly, the opinions of female members of the new generation interviewed vary greatly, ranging from defiance, framed both in a modernist and in a radical religious way, to resignation and acquiescence. For the small number of self-defined 'modernists', expressing defiance means questioning the veracity of the authorities' religious dictates, especially the restrictive practices of the *mutaw'a*, members of the Committee for the Propagation of Good and the Forbidding of Evil. Although these modernists still see themselves as operating within an Islamic discourse, they challenge the application of the *shari'a* (Islamic law) to modern Saudi Arabia. The second position from which a defiant critique is launched is from within the discourse of the religious authorities themselves. This critique aligns itself positively with the symbolism of the veil and the rules of gender segregation but seeks to build and deploy a female Islamic solidarity to call for greater freedom within the teachings of Islam. The attitudes of the women of the new generation embody the clash of tradition and modernity facing Saudi Arabia today.

They seek to understand and mediate the controversies and contradictions that arise as they begin to define a new identity in a changing world.

As was noted previously, the family unit remains the centre of the new generation's world – and the stable basis of identity for all youth, both male and female, continues to be familial. For example, Amina (18), from Jeddah, has a desire to be a lawyer but wants to be a wife and mother first. 'This', she says, 'is because the family is something lasting, more than a career or law degree.'

The centrality of the family means that even after marriage women do not change their paternal surname. The behaviour of young people, good or bad, is associated primarily with the family of their birth. Their actions will continue to honour or shame their patrilineal kin irrespective of their age. This means that the independent identity of a wife is expressed not only in keeping her own name but also (since there is no concept of joint property in Islamic marriage) in retaining the independence of her finances. On the other hand, the young women interviewed are keenly aware of their legal and social dependence on their guardians: their fathers from birth and then their husbands after marriage. This fact is exemplified by a young woman's inability to acquire an independent *tab'iyya* (civil status card). Instead, legally she is added to her father's identity card when born and transferred to her husband's when married. In fact, she is treated as an extension of her male guardian in many areas of her social and legal existence. As a result, her individual freedoms are curtailed in many areas of life. Particularly telling, perhaps, is the fact that women cannot exit the country without the written permission of their male guardians.

The interviews indicate that new forms of thinking about gender and the role of women in Saudi society are emerging among both male and female members of the new generation. Gender as the stable and un-questioned component of identity is no longer taken for granted. The roles women are expected to play as obedient wives, self-sacrificing mothers and diligent housewives are coming under challenge from expectations for greater equality, educational advancement and career aspirations. Nearly all those interviewed have mothers who are 'housewives', whereas the new generation aspires to pursue careers and fulfil the expectations that education has raised. Some question the apparent inequality in the educational system and the limitations in career choices. However, as with the centrality of Islam, and the specific local, legal interpretation of it, all those interviewed were also keenly aware of the limits of traditional social constraints. Career choices are limited to those socially and officially defined as 'suitable' for women. Teaching is a good example of a socially acceptable career. This is a respectable job for women, a job which brings high social status. With its convenient working hours and long holidays it allows women to combine work with having children and family responsibilities. Medicine is another respectable career for women. Although demanding in terms of working hours it has become a highly prestigious occupation.

Hind (18) highlights how a woman may balance ambition with cultural constraints. She wants to become a paediatrician and practise medicine in one of the local Jeddah hospitals. She frames her desire to enter the medical profession within the boundaries of tradition. For example, she does not foresee travelling abroad to attend a conference to expand her knowledge. 'That would not be possible.' Overall, Hind does not believe that Saudi women, even medical doctors, can become international citizens because of the societal barriers they face. These barriers mean that culturally unacceptable occupations, such as those of lawyers, engineers or airline pilots, remain a dream for young ambitious women within the present Saudi society.

Where education is concerned the majority of women interviewed are realistic about their choice of studies. They acknowledge that there is a narrower range of academic and vocational courses and career paths available to them than to men. When attending colleges in Saudi Arabia, young women tend to compromise between what they are capable of academically and socially acceptable career paths. However, changes in the economy are opening up new areas of possibility and in some cases a necessity for female employment. Ambiguous categories of jobs, such as that of computer analyst, are emerging in these changing circumstances. However, even if in practice such professions open up new avenues they are nonetheless viewed suspiciously by the more conservative. In any case, employment outside the home, albeit in a gender-segregated environment, means women altering set patterns and routines and unsettling traditional identities. In this changing environment new gender boundaries will inevitably be created.

Economic change as a result of the advent of oil changed the socio-economic position of Saudi women. The majority of the interviewees' grandmothers would have been involved in traditional modes of production such as agro-pastoralism. This meant that domestic life and economic production were combined and centred on the extended family unit in the pre-oil era. As changes in the economy took place at the time of the mothers' generation, the traditional occupations became marginalized in an increasingly national economy integrated in global commerce. This led to the majority of urban women (especially members of the new middle class) becoming housewives, a process that removed them from direct input into the generation of family income. The oil-driven rise in living standards certainly provided modern consumer comforts and high levels of health care. But for the growing numbers of Saudi women living in urban centres it reduced social interaction, refocusing their lives in the domestic sphere, the company of other women and the extended family.

The young people interviewed express a growing consciousness of a dichotomy between the education that young women receive and the roles they are expected to play in society. There is also a marked difference of opinion between the young women and men about the implications of a decline in oil revenues. The latter are concerned about finding occupations that are up to the standards of their fathers' generation while the former focus on the possibilities that changing economic circumstances may bring. If living standards are measured not only on a material basis but also on the quality of life in which choices are available to the population, then many young women who benefited from the expansion in education want to carry these benefits into their adult lives. This would involve having smaller families and the ability to choose their own careers.

For those interviewed, identity, status and future roles are open to renegotiation to a degree which previous generations of women could not have believed. The interviewees are generally very much aware of these new possibilities. They have their own ideas about what is worth altering or retaining. For example, Dunya (15), from Medina, thinks: 'Women in Saudi Arabia are over-dependent. They depend on drivers because they are not allowed to do things themselves.' She believes that there is more hope for those who are most open-minded and who demand freedom. 'Freedom is important and it is acquired while studying abroad. One's mentality becomes broad, especially for women who are so restricted in Saudi Arabia.' It is obvious from what Dunya says that exposure through education and travel increases the awareness of young women about inequality and heightens their demands for freedom.

Nevertheless, the young women interviewed are also aware and keen to preserve the stability of a society that provides certainties. They see themselves as willing members of extended families which are patri-archal. They centre themselves within this patriarchal family structure because it is all that they have known. In a country where there is no guaranteed employment or protection by the state, the family remains the centre of their world. However, continuous geographical and social mobility means it is inevitable that the perception of the extended family unit is altering, and the dynamics of the relationships are taking on new forms, for example in attitudes and behaviour between spouses.

One of the main characteristics of the contemporary political situation is that the issue of women's rights and behaviour has been placed at the centre of a potential power struggle between the *'ulama* and the state.[1] The state uses the role of women within society to make symbolic gestures to confirm its commitment to Islam, for example by enforcing the wearing of the veil and the legal ban on women driving cars and by limiting the choice young women have in education and career choices, thus preserving the strict gender segregation in all public spheres. The dominant impression of Saudi life is a lack of women in public places; the main cities appear to be populated exclusively by men. The symbolism of the veil to Islamic identity filters down through society and is sometimes echoed by the youth. When Faris (16) marries, he wants his wife to be a *muhajjaba* (the practice whereby women cover the body and hair, except for the face and hands). 'All Muslim women must wear the *hijab*, the women's veil, especially if they go abroad, for example to the United States. This is not because of conservative Islamic beliefs, but rather as a question of identity.' The young women interviewed expressed opinions on these issues ranging from anger and frustration to resignation and acceptance.

---

[1] Saddika Arebi, *Women and Words in Saudi Arabia* (New York: Columbia University Press, 1994), pp. 13 and 15.

Cultural and religious perceptions of patriarchy

Islam is woven into the normative fabric of the whole region and forms the basis of the ideological rationale for women's education and participation. Yet, although interpretations of 'correct' Islamic behaviour influence all sections of society, local customs, norms and tribal traditions actually dictate women's roles and are enforced through familial structures. In recent years, this shifting collection of traditions has been deployed to enforce the psycho-social power of men over women. The *ulama's* power also continues to play a significant role in determining political legitimacy and the role of women in relation to it.

In sum, while Islam provides an ideological basis for social life in Saudi Arabia, the family unit is intrinsic to its order and manifestation. Within the extended familial structure lies a predominant patrilinear, patrilocal and patriarchal pattern enforced by tribal values of honour and shame. Although migration into urban areas has encouraged the growth of the nuclear family, the extended family structure remains a powerful force in identity construction and social organization. For instance, a woman is given the right to protection through the concept of *iltizam* (obligation). This means roughly that her father, husband, brothers and male cousins are responsible for her welfare rather than she herself. *Iltizam* exempts the mother from the pressures of having to support a family and to leave the home for the workplace. Fahda (15), from Riyadh, believes that the traditional centrality of the family is to be cherished; it 'honours women who can sit at home in the shelter of their families'.

Women's welfare is not directly a state but a family responsibility; the social burden of the 'welfare mother' appears to be negligible in Saudi Arabia. Despite the decline in oil revenues since the 1980s the Saudi state would not expect a rise in the number of female-headed families, as in Western and some African countries. Although this economic buffer eliminates single-parent homes, retains the family unit and provides relative security for women, its very essence impinges on a woman's freedom. In practical terms, *iltizam* justifies the suppression of women at all levels of social interaction under the guise of preserving a woman's honour. Men are expected to provide for dependent women and children, with women bearing the enormous responsibility of rearing on average five children. The husband is obliged by *iltizam* to supervise all household expenses.

The wife makes only one-third of food purchases and the husband makes all purchases of durable commodities, including the satellite dish. Therefore, although 95 per cent of households own a television and 60–70 per cent a stereo or video, the patriarchal character of society is maintained.[2] Since paternalism is a common feature in patrilineal authoritarian regimes, the state's attitude towards women also becomes an extension of family control.

The Saudi government is beginning to make decisions on state-sponsored welfare programmes which could lead to substantial cultural shifts regarding the work ethic of both men and women. Although changes are taking place through policy revision and resource management/ development, educational policy remains the crucial vehicle for continuity and change. Islam again provides the normative basis, with the relevant *hadith* (sayings of the prophet Muhammad) supporting investment in education as the basis for positive social development. Despite the expansion of the educational programmes variances remain in the system's treatment of female students and teachers.

The gender divide

The separation of the sexes is strictly applied in all public spheres, schools, universities, shops, restaurants, banks and even lifts in some buildings. Ideally, the two sexes never meet outside the home after kindergarten, with courtship forbidden and marriages arranged. Young women stay at home and learn 'domestic virtues', while boys opt for a career.

Gender acts as a material and ideational dividing line throughout the Saudi education system. Formal teaching at private and state schools is segregated and takes place in separate buildings, with different teachers. The extent of this gender divide has grown alongside the development of education in Saudi Arabia. As already noted, the first secular schools for young men were given names such as *falah* (Success), in sharp contrast to women's secular schools, which were not only opened much later but given names such as *dar al-hanan* (House of Tenderness), supposedly in keeping with feminine 'nature'. As the names suggest, the objectives for

[2] The Saudi-British Bank, The HSBC Group: Business Profile Series, *Saudi Arabia*, 6th edn, 3rd quarter, 1994, p. 15.

pursuing an education were regarded differently for men and women, not simply because of male conservatism but because women were perceived as operating within a different society from men.

The growth of higher education has led to most universities admitting Muslim pupils from both sexes. Large numbers of women now attend universities in Saudi Arabia's main cities, albeit in separately assigned areas. However, three of the main universities (Imam Muhammad bin Saud Islamic University in Riyadh, the University of Petroleum and Minerals and the Islamic University of Medina) do not admit women. In the rest, women are barred from such fields as geology, petroleum engineering and law. They are taught by female lecturers only and in the absence of female specialists women can only be taught by men through the medium of closed-circuit television. This segregation has led to women receiving inferior scientific equipment and inadequate access to proper laboratory facilities. Since the early 1990s economic decline has contributed to further cuts in facilities in the female sections of the universities. Nevertheless, the number of female students continues to rise.

Many women from the merchant families and from the educated classes have gone overseas (to Jordan, Egypt, the United States or the United Kingdom) for a university education. There, they are free to choose any discipline and are able to become more confident in their ability to change their status and position when they return home. During the 1980s, with greater stress on the Saudi-ization policy, enrolment in local universities was encouraged. Although choice may be less extensive, the process of empowerment remains. The process of the gradual expansion of domestic educational opportunities for women culminated in the opening of a private college for girls in Jeddah in 1998. It offers up-to-date educational methods, but at a high cost. Wherever the location of study, women of this new generation, unlike their mothers, face a widening gap between traditional familial-social roles as 'housewife' and 'mother' and the educational experiences both at home and abroad which encourage aspirations that patriarchal family and social customs restrain.

Society is divided not only according to gender but also hierarchically according to wealth and lineage. This issue has become extenuated among the upper-class women interviewed who have had to study in the Kingdom. Several women complained about the mixing of social classes. The richest women from 'liberal' families can go abroad. However, those who cannot complained about having to mix with women they view as their social inferiors. In the hierarchically stratified society of Saudi Arabia, and until the opening of universities, women rarely mixed with other women outside their class or network of families; in contrast, men from different societal backgrounds have always mixed through public careers. When women are abroad, cross-class encounters take place in a different context and are not viewed in the same way as in the strictly regulated and self-conscious Saudi society.

Legitimate role models and the growth of Islamic feminism

Most women interviewed want definite change in their social circumstances, especially when compared with the young men from the same families or from similar social backgrounds. These young men are concerned that they maintain their fathers' position in the family and society. They link the maintenance of this position to the continuance of clearly defined public and private gender roles. Women's definitions of 'traditional' roles have changed. But their experiences of the rapid social transformation of Saudi society are shaped by the search for an authentic identity coherent with traditional Muslim culture, yet consistent with their desire to capitalize on increased opportunities. Their choices have widened but their role models remain derived from traditional culture and the traditional sources of women's power. There have been few women in Saudi society with a public role to look up to, therefore young women take as their role models Islamic historical figures such as A'isha and Khadija and others among the *ummahat al mu'minin* (mothers of the believers). They frequently quote the Prophet's saying: 'Learn half of your religion from that red-headed one!' – referring to A'isha's example of virtue and learning for all people. A'isha was a major religious authority and in modern times a symbol for feminists in Muslim/Arab countries. By contrast, Khadija – the Prophet's first wife – is the archetypal businesswoman who successfully continued her activities after marriage and even employed her husband, and she thus provides a role model for economic equality. Therefore, the just distribution of wealth and power between the sexes is not simply an ideological goal to which a community aspires but the economic foundation on which it should be based.

According to *shari'a*, there is no distinction between a man and a woman from the legal age of sixteen in terms of ownership, control and use of money. A woman is entitled to *nafaqa* (maintenance after divorce or separation),[3] and she has full control over her *mahr* (dower), her share of the inheritance and other financial securities. These general Islamic foundations for equality act as inspiration for the recently educated female members of the new generation.

It has been argued that the challenging and questioning of women's roles and status in their own society in their own terms is a form of feminism.[4] However, feminism as a political and social force has been commonly attributed to Western liberal principles of individual human rights, democracy and freedom. The spread of suffrage movements across Europe in the nineteenth and early twentieth centuries and the rise of militant feminism in the United States all testify to this vision. There is a feeling among Muslim feminists that their culturally and geographically specific movement sets a new and uncharted agenda for social development. This leads to a rejection of Western feminism or at least its radical modification for different cultural and historical circumstances. The ideology of Islamic feminism calls for the promotion of the inalienable rights of women voiced through the moral framework of the Quran and the *hadith*, doctrines which call for the judicious treatment of women. Since powerful women such as A'isha existed in early Islamic Arabia, Islamic feminists claim that their movement calls on a heritage which existed in varying forms throughout Islamic history across Muslim communities, whether East or West. The *hijab*, for example, has become for some Muslim women a symbol of solidarity and not necessarily of repression, and has become widespread from the streets of Malaysia to Egypt,[5] often through personal choice. In Saudi Arabia, however, the black veil is an official requirement for women. But here too some women choose to adopt a stricter version than that imposed by the authorities, wearing it at all times. The new veiling is an example of a revival of

---

[3] Mai Yamani, 'Introduction', in Mai Yamani (ed.), *Feminism and Islam: Legal and Literary Perspectives* (London: Ithaca Press, 1996).

[4] Ibid.

[5] See Arlene E. MacLeod, *Accommodating Protest: Working Women, the New Veiling, and Change in Cairo* (New York: Columbia University Press, 1991).

tradition, a symbol or sign of Islam but also an attempt to create an Islamic feminism.

The conflicts and pressures that change brings are deepened by reference to a modernized West. There is an obvious search for a modernity that is distinctive from the West. This changing perception among women has found its most vocal outlet in Islamic feminism. The use of Islamic terminology and attire means women's demands for increased access to education and work can be voiced in terms not seen as alien to the society. The anchoring of these demands in Islamic language has given them widespread resonance among the female members of the educated class, the new middle class and also those of rural origins who have recently become urbanized. The Islamic motif cuts across class barriers.

The disjunction between educational experiences and the exclusion of women from the workforce has driven the growth and popular appeal of the Islamic feminist movement. Beginning in the universities, this movement was nurtured by lecturers who were influenced by Egyptian ideas on women's Muslim rights. The movement spread rapidly, with gatherings led by charismatic leaders. In their meetings, numbering as many as 300, these women remained veiled to represent their solidarity and their commitment to Islam. This distinguishes the new Islamic feminists from the traditional attitude whereby women veiled only when in public; it also distinguishes the Islamic feminists from liberal protesters who have less support within an Islamic society. The political programme of these young feminists has not yet been clearly defined. They do not demand the right to vote or to work with men. However, their leading members are at the forefront of the public professions that are open to women, such as women's branches of banks and the universities. Therefore, although women in this group clearly represent the educated new generation, the Islamic discourse provides them with a moral power to challenge patriarchal norms that stand in the way of their professional achievements. The aggressive attitude is a significant distinction between the new women and those of the same generation who have accepted the traditional role of women in the family. Thus the appearance of Islamic attire belies a new and even modern attitude of women in relation to education, employment and private life. Some of the most vocal and ambitious women interviewed kept their *hijab* and spoke in an Islamic language strongly based on Quranic and *hadith* sayings.

The young female population pose a conscious and unconscious threat to the status quo, notably with regard to social and religious change but also economic change, specifically the problems of the Saudi-ization of the workforce. The requirements of the global economy create tensions with the existing norms that keep women at home. Resistance by the more conservative sections of Saudi society to adapting traditional concepts of women's employment to fit the norms of a dynamic global community is posing a problem. The tension between these two positions is coming to the fore because large numbers of women are increasingly aware of the argument by other educated Muslim women that Islam gives them legal and social rights. The new female generation has also become aware, through media and travel, of Saudi Arabia's religious conservatism relative to other GCC countries, let alone the wider Muslim world and Europe.

The concept of personal choice

For the first time in the three generations of Saudi history, education and wider cultural exposure have given the new generation the tools to analyse and question the foundations and scope of gender roles. Unlike their grandmothers and mothers, women of this new generation have to decide on the purpose of education in their lives – whether it will enhance the wife/mother function dictated by familial and social norms or offer them career opportunities. The men of the new generation also have to decide on their attitude to the position and role of women. They are still dominant, and they have to choose either to continue to restrain or to encourage the aspirations that education has evoked in their sisters and wives.

According to US State Department figures,[6] Saudi women represent 55 per cent of university graduates in Saudi Arabia. Most of the young girls interviewed between the ages of fifteen and eighteen aspire to go to university. The motivations behind this aspiration vary widely. Some want to improve their future career prospects, while others value the undoubted social prestige and status attached to university qualifications. Still others see it as a pleasant way to pass the time until they receive a

[6] See US Department of State Report, March 1996.

proposal of marriage. Their attitudes fall into three broad categories: studying for its own sake, studying for a profession, and compromise – combining studies with familial social circumstances. But overall the women interviewed consider higher education their right as Saudi citizens. Jobs, on the other hand, are often explained in relation to their social significance or acceptability. New jobs should not be threatening to their family and community. These women understand and for the large part conform to the boundaries imposed by social norms. They place their life choices within these social norms.

Haifa (16), from Riyadh, is keen to go to university in Saudi Arabia because she wants to study children's education. She loves children and feels that teaching others is part of her religious and national duty. Haifa, in aspiring to pursue a teaching career, is conforming to a culturally acceptable path that will not clash with her aspiration to get married and have numerous children. Hiba (15) wants to go to university to study computer science. But she is realistic about how she will use this skill in later life. She doubts that she will be able to work after leaving college; she just wants to study because it is 'the thing to do'. She does not envisage job opportunities for women. For her, the potential for women working is vague, especially when combined with family responsibilities. Because of the restrictions she sees for women within Saudi society she makes a distinction between studying and a profession; one does not necessarily lead to the other. For Hiba and others interviewed education is a source of social status, but a career is not necessarily the objective. Abir (15) says that she is influenced more by her family than by her education. Her ultimate ambition is 'to become a teacher'. Her choice, she reveals, is influenced by both the local traditions and the standards dictated for suitable female jobs.

On the other hand, Maha (17), who is a *muhajjaba* (i.e. she covers the body and hair, except for face and hands), is much more active in pursuing her goals. She wants to complete her secondary education and then study interior design. She thinks that studying in a foreign country is 'a big effort'. However, it is necessary 'because Saudi women have regressed … we must study so that we can influence others'. Maha's ambitions are not limited to succeeding in her studies. She sees the restrictive role women have in Saudi society and wants to overcome this and lead by example. She chose interior design because she will be able to pursue this without breaking social taboos. She will be able to work with other women in their homes in the context of segregated Saudi society.

Manal (17) has one more year of secondary education. She loves art and drawing. Manal wants to study architecture and believes that she will have to compromise: 'We have so many aspirations, but many things are forbidden because of *kalam an-nas* (people's gossip).' For her too, interior design will enable her to work in the domestic private sphere without coming into contact with members of the opposite sex who are not from her immediate family.

Maryam (27) from Jeddah, graduated from King Abdul Aziz University, after which she spent three years as a social worker in a hospital and helped with her maternal family's business. After much debate within the extended family, Maryam went to the United States for postgraduate studies in psychology and special education. She arrived at the decision because of her autistic ten-year-old cousin and because she sought the patronage of her influential uncle who had previously employed her in his organization. Maryam's work with children is in line with the perceived 'nature of women' as carers and nurturers and the traditional belief that working with handicapped children is an honour-able job. Moreover, schools for the handicapped are also segregated, and only mothers attend parent–teacher meetings about their daughters. For Maryam, having a career is not necessarily a political or a controversial action; rather it reflects cultural norms about the nurturing role of women in society.

Malak, a young *muhajjaba*, does not see herself as a career woman. She said that most of her teenage friends were already engaged to be married, conforming with the customary practice, but this was only for material or practical reasons. For Malak, marriage and motherhood are a form of *'ibada* (worship). This is probably a reflection not of traditional or customary beliefs but of her own spiritual or religious idealism.

Ashwaq (15) is an example of the new generation of young women who increasingly feel the restrictions which society places upon them. Ashwaq's passion is archaeology. It is her long-held ambition to go to university and become an archaeologist. However, she acknowledges that after graduation she will be forced to become a teacher. This is because as a woman she will not be able to travel or go on digs. Ashwaq's sense of the limitation of women's choices is very pronounced. Aware of the massive social constraints she faces in trying to fulfil her ambition, her opinion understandably fluctuates between defiance and acceptance.

Jamila (21), like Ashwaq, acknowledges the constraints she faces within Saudi society. She plans to take the exit option and wants to marry a Saudi man who lives in the United States. This is the only way she feels she will be able to study abroad for her Master's degree in jewellery design. When she is married she wants to have three sons. She does not want to have any daughters 'because girls have a very hard time in Saudi Arabia; they basically have no future'.

Dania (24) is a good example of the coexistence of change and tradition in the identity of the new generation. She is sure she will get married, 'as soon as she finishes her education'. Dania is aware that marriage will delay her studies; she says that she will have less space, especially if her future husband is *namati* (set in his ways). She says: 'I will choose my own husband, but will make the choice suitable for my society and my family.' While on the one hand she aspires to independence of choice, on the other she is actually conforming to the wishes and expectations of society and family.

Suhair (27) is from Najran. Her ambition in life is to be a good mother and to give her two children 'all they need, and to protect them'. When asked about striking a balance between the demands of family relationships and her general aspirations, she answered that her extended family have many requirements, but they understand that she is with her husband and children. Suhair approves of male–female encounters prior to marriage. She has no intention of having any more children, although her husband desires more. This decision is based on how much time and care she can give her children.

Hiba (15) says: 'There is no freedom of choice for work in Saudi Arabia for a woman.' Asked whether there is a clash between tradition and her expectations, she said, 'Yes, women are treated differently from men. Women have to study, but they cannot study together with men.' She believes there is a clash between modernity and traditional segregation. Despite being more rebellious, Hiba sees the general circumstances in her country as acceptable.

Thamer (15) asserts that he will marry a Saudi Arabian woman who will only work if her job is compatible with his and with raising the children, or is an occupation which serves the nation, like teaching. Otherwise, in his view, a wife should stay at home and prepare lunch because taking care of the home is her primary duty. The difficulty is if she has a job while her husband does not have one. 'I will marry her to have children, not for her profession or her money. There are people who marry a woman for her money.' Thamer expresses here an awareness of the threat of unemployment and economic pressures that are undermining the designated roles of husbands and wives.

Economic leeway

Women as individual entrepreneurs have been increasingly active in the private sector but less so in the public sector. Informed sources from *al-khidma al-madaniyya* (the civil service) claim that women participate in most professions, such as medicine, teaching and administration. But mirroring certain educational practices, they are excluded from legal and political sectors. Jobs remain strictly segregated according to government orders and social expectations. According to estimates by the *Middle East Executive Reports,* around 40 per cent of Saudi private wealth is in female hands.[7] According to the *Saudi Gazette* 15,000 Saudi commercial establishments are owned by women, and the Chamber of Commerce in Riyadh, Jeddah and Dhahran include more than 5,000 women members.[8] This is a result of women's economic capacity under the *shari'a*. Saudi women are increasingly aware of this capacity and the more affluent consider the separation of property and finances in marriage to be their trump card. They are aware that money is power and perhaps the only means to empowerment accessible to them in Saudi Arabia, given employment restrictions. But this economic capacity simultaneously venerates and isolates women. As noted above, commerce and trade remain the most prominently segregated environments, with women's banks and shops, owned, managed and patronized by women only. Saudi women are stretching themselves beyond the moulds of boutique owner and hairdresser to import/export businesses or banking. Yet a woman is not allowed by tradition to enter the Ministry of Commerce,

[7] *Middle East Executive Reports*, Vol. 5, No. 5, 1982, p. 22.
[8] *Saudi Gazette*, 23 October 1998.

even to comply with the necessary formalities of conducting business. A *wakil shar'i* (a male with power of attorney) has to do the necessary paperwork for her.

The gender distinctions are also evident in the consumer sector. Not only are there special branches of banks for women, but most banks offer different bank cards for men, women and the young (those under twenty-five). These distinctions are taken for granted by the youth. All the big malls have shops designated for women, with signs clearly saying 'For women only. Men are not allowed.'

Empowerment outside the home contradicts traditional concepts of honour and shame. These are directly challenged when women work outside the home, especially if they can come into contact with non-*mihrims* (male relatives). However, these concepts have evolved and may be modified in accordance with economic need. In Saudi Arabia, the inclusion of women in the workforce could become a major strand of the indigenization policy.

One attempt at women's participation comes in the form of economic and personal charity work. *Al-jam'iyya al-khayriyya* (The Charitable Organization) and *al-jam'iyya al-faysaliyya* (Faisal's (charitable) Organization) cater for socially disadvantaged women and children and are patronized and directed by wealthy women. The latter currently supports 6,000 families around the country. Donors offer money through *sadaqa* (alms-giving), *zakat* (the Islamic tax system) and *zakat al-fitr* (the levy at the end of Ramadan). The professionals in the organization locate the poor and distribute the donations. They also manage and supervise *arbita,* long-term charity housing for abandoned women, including widowed, divorced or elderly unmarried women who find themselves either with no relative or abandoned by relatives – essentially those women who cannot take shelter under the protection of *iltizam.* Charitable enterprises are partly subsidized and supported by the government, which backs this aspect of women's work. So charity has become the central objective of gatherings of elite women, whose wealth comes both from family and from their own business enterprises. The plight of the poor has been adopted by educated affluent Saudi women desiring to make an impact on their community within an Islamic and Arab framework. Several women interviewed have been voluntarily working in a charitable organization. For these women, social work via charity is a means of empowering themselves where both custom and law marginalize the participation of women at the decision-making level. Within these restrictions, status and respectability are achieved in an 'Islamic' context through 'honourable' jobs. This is the first step towards bridging the gap between education and employment.

The socially defined limits of change

The choices the new generation face in defining their gender identity appear vast when compared with those of the previous generations. The interviewees clearly recognize the limitations imposed on them by the state, the religious authorities and traditional beliefs, as well as their families. There is little uniformity of perception or commonality of viewpoint concerning gender segregation, polygamy and veiling. These issues are viewed differently, according to socio-economic background, education and experience of other cultures. Hence, there are those who appear to be struggling with these practices, while others accept the constraints and seek to justify them.

All the young women interviewed are aware of the limitations the traditional patriarchal system places on them. Their opinions range from acceptance to compromise and in rare cases rebellion. Several men, especially from the new middle class, expressed approval of gender segregation. They saw it as a key part of Saudi Arabian tradition that should not be altered for fear of creating *fitna* (provocation leading to chaos). Sultan (15) thought all Muslim women should wear the *hijab* and pointedly asked why I (as a Muslim woman) was not wearing one when outside the Kingdom. This opinion was also expressed by Mansour (30), who believes that gender segregation in all educational and professional spheres is an essential part of Saudi culture. Abdul Karim (23) believes that Saudi traditions are good for society and that the segregation of the sexes in educational and professional spheres, as well as the veil, should be maintained. He believes that it is better for women not to drive: 'I would never allow my mother to drive. How can she do that with the veil?' As for his wife working, he said: 'The minute a woman works she forgets about her home.' What underlies his thoughts, and those of several others from the new middle class, is fear. Some believed that men and women should be separated on moral grounds: 'Do you want us to compromise our identity and expose our women like Westerners do? How could we ever marry a woman who has been already exposed in cinemas or other public places?'

The attitude of the women interviewed varied. Several *muhajjabat* displayed a conservative approach. They agreed to the segregation of the sexes in educational spheres, but the younger and more liberal considered this separation, excluding women from the better jobs and from access to better facilities, to be unfair. Hiba (15), from Medina, thinks: 'Women are treated differently from men because of traditional beliefs. Women have to study, but they cannot study together with men.' She believes there is a difficult clash between modern requirements and traditional segregation. Unsurprisingly, it was the women and especially the young with exposure to the West who articulated provocative and often rebellious ideas about the segregation of the sexes.

Asma (28), from Jeddah, talked about the beneficial effects of letting young people of both sexes mix socially before marriage. This is happening with greater frequency among the middle classes. One of the new trends is to hold supervised 'DJ' parties for young people. Asma said that she approved of certain mothers agreeing to these mixed parties and that it was 'unnatural for a hundred girls in a room to dance with one another'. This, she warned, 'can trigger lesbianism'. She also thinks that 'DJ' parties provide a good meeting place for future husbands 'because everyone is of the same *mustawa* (socio-economic level)'. She said that these 'DJ' parties had been going on for three years with beneficial results (she has had more exposure to Western culture, satellite television, magazines and books etc. than some of the girls from the new middle class interviewed). Asma's definitions of sexual categories and fears of their transgression have been solidified by exposure to Western stereotypes of gender roles. Traditionally women's parties were single-sex and homosexuality was rarely an issue. However, the acceptance of Western definitions of sexuality are raising previously unconsidered concerns about sexual boundaries.

I asked Ahlam, Amel, Jamila and Asia whether they thought women should drive. They collectively exclaimed: 'We would love to drive. Unfortunately this is not possible.' Amel explained, 'We have to be realistic and live with it. The authorities link driving to religion; furthermore, we would not be able to handle men's aggressive behaviour.' This last comment refers to the courting ritual of young male drivers who chase and signal to women they see in parallel cars. Dana (15), from Medina, expressed similar sentiments: 'The authorities should give us more chances; a woman must drive a car.' But for her this was not only an issue of equality, it was also for the good of the whole country. Women should drive 'so that we get rid of the foreign drivers and help the process of Saudi-ization as well as get more freedom for women'. Dana has framed her own arguments in the practical problem-solving language of the government. It would be rational for women to drive because it would help the government to meet their key policy on indigenization of the workforce. She is concerned about Saudi-ization, but, underneath, her main concern is for greater personal freedom.

Adnan (24), when asked whether he would object to his wife working, said: 'As long as she does her first job, which is taking care of myself and my home, cooking etc. and my children.' When asked whether the genders should be segregated in educational and professional spheres, he described the practice as 'backward. ... The origins of this have nothing to do with religion. It is more associated with the cultural practices of the Bedouin.' Adnan is of urban Hijazi descent and frequently makes the distinction between the more strict Nejdi social practices and the cosmopolitan approach of the Hijaz. But because Adnan sees himself as a good Muslim the practices he disagrees with have to be classified as social in origin and not religious. He cited *ayyam al-sahaba* (days of the prophet's companions) as proof that such gender segregation did not exist in the prophet's time. When asked which aspects of Saudi tradition he most objected to, Adnan again referred to the segregation between men and women. He said that this was but one of 'many aspects which isolate women from playing an effective role in society. Women should participate; they make up half of the society, but nonetheless the door is closed in their face because of this ridiculous practice.'

Saad (16) asked what 'encounters' between men and women meant. For him, encounters before marriage allowed by religion are good, but what is not allowed is bad. He would not approve of sexual relations before marriage, 'but there are different standards; for men it is approved of but not for women'. Saad expresses a conservative view; he overtly agrees with gender segregation but, like others, beneath this acceptance he does not really agree.

Noura (16), whose father works for Saudia Airlines, lived in London for several years, returning to Saudi Arabia for holidays. She believes that 'there is a *katma* (suffocation) closing up on girls in most families. While the boys have more rights and freedom, the girls are told that everything is shameful and sinful. But boys also have problems; they cannot go anywhere – there are no places for leisure like cinemas in Saudi Arabia.' Dunya (15) has regularly travelled abroad. Dunya believes that if they allow women to fly an aeroplane or work in tourism, Saudi Arabia will modernize and progress faster. 'It will be better for the country.' Manal (17) says that women have so many aspirations, but many things are forbidden because of *kalam an-nas* (gossip). She believes that society is progressing rapidly, therefore eventually 'women must drive because we have evolved'.

With the dynamic interactions between modernity and tradition and the confusing and contradictory choices facing the new generation, there is bound to be evidence of tension between social certainties and possibilities for wider choice, and between different sections of society with different perceptions. This tension is especially visible in the different and changing expectations both men and women bring to marriage. A symptom of these changing expectations is the rapidly increasing divorce rate. Official Saudi statistics report that 24 per cent of marriages end in divorce. The Ministry of Justice calculates that in 1997, 64,329 marriages were recorded and in the same year 15,697 divorces were registered. It is noteworthy that the highest divorce rates took place in Mecca and the second highest in Riyadh.[9] Women with family support are demanding that they include *'isma* – the right to obtain a divorce as a condition of the marriage contract. These conditions usually reflect their desire to continue studying or the objection to their husband taking a second wife. When these promises are broken divorce is considered the only way to obtain a better life. Unlike their male counterparts, women expressed throughout the interviews demands for a better quality of life than their mothers'. Ahlam has just divorced her husband at the age of eighteen because he refused to let her work. She was able to divorce him because her family had included the right to divorce in the marriage contract if Ahlam were unable to continue her studies. Increasingly

[9] See *Al-Qabas,* 17 August 1999.

women are asking for the *'isma* while Saudi men are reluctant to grant it. In Ahlam's case, when her husband resisted her choice of a more public social role, she sought her father's permission to divorce. 'I am ambitious,' she explains, 'I cannot just sit at home.'

Sahar (30), from Jeddah, divorced three years ago after a marriage that lasted seven years. She has one son, aged seven, who 'is always with me'. Although the law of custody specifies that a boy of seven should go to his father, in Sahar's case the agreement is that she can keep her son as long as she does not remarry. After her divorce, when Sahar was 'depressed', her father introduced her to one of the medical doctors who worked with him at Saudia Airlines. He advised her to work in order to combat the depression. She approves of male–female encounters prior to marriage; she had met her husband before marrying him and had fallen in love with him. However, the problem that occurred later was caused by his fear of taking the responsibilities of being a father and a husband.

Sundus (23) explained that her ex-husband was so strict about all her movements and ideas that she looked back at the three years of her marriage as years of 'suffering a traditional, religious way of thinking'. Finally, when he refused to grant her any freedom she felt forced to ask for a divorce.

Among some of the young women interviewed there was great frustration that their aspirations, nurtured by education and foreign travel, could not be fulfilled within Saudi Arabia. Two of the female interviewees from families dependent on state employment railed against the sexism inherent in the present Saudi system. Dunya (15) has an ambition to become the first Saudi woman pilot, 'but it is almost impossible. If we cannot drive how can we fly?' Therefore she feels she has few options open to her. 'What can I do,' she says, 'but study mathematics until I die?'

The expectation of change constrained by socialization means that young women increasingly express role expectations that are ambiguous. Amina (18) wants to study law, despite the fact that there are no women lawyers in Saudi Arabia. 'By the time I graduate I hope there will be opportunities to practise law. I hope things will move, otherwise I will start it.' She wants to earn her own income and not be dependent on her husband. She says that her year of education in the United Kingdom taught her to depend on herself, but she also values the virtues of self-control and respect for Saudi society. She intends to be a wife and mother first because 'the family is something lasting'. Interestingly, although she wants to change some aspects of her role, she says she expects her husband to fulfil the customary *iltizam* of maintaining the household. 'My money will not go towards maintaining the house.' Finally, she expects she will get her job through contacts: 'Contacts will get you there.' Amina is apparently unaware of the inherent contradiction in her statement. She wants to be an innovator and gain more freedom for her life choices but does not see her dependence on private and public patriarchal structures, the use of *iltizam* and contacts as threatening or constraining her.

Women face many other obstacles; they are still subject to the aggressive attentions of men in public places. The customary male approach of *ghazal* (romantic flattery) to establish a relationship is prevalent. This is perceived by some young women as *mu'akasa* (an intrusion) and as a means of establishing male power and dominance. Others are merely excited or confused by the practice. Men like to protect their wives from exposure to the opposite sex. For instance, Said aspired to marry a beautiful and educated woman who would not wish to work, although he said, at least to me, that he was open to the idea if that was what she wanted. Generally, in the educated class men claimed to be open to the idea of women working; however, at this stage of economic development additional income from a working wife is not a pressing issue. The preference is still to maintain the traditional role of provider. This attitude may change with education and with the deterioration of the economic situation once there is a need for women to supplement the family income. Sami said that he wanted to marry an educated woman who was 'next to me rather than behind me'. He expected that he would meet her not through an arranged marriage but at a mixed party: 'Someone will arrange a meeting for me. It is like a blind date.' He is not in a hurry to marry because he does not want 'to choose a bride and then choose another one afterwards'. Faiz said that he would marry at twenty-five and have four children, but he would not object if his wife wanted to work. He said his mother would choose his bride for him.

Through their encounters with the outside world, both at first hand and through the media, the youth have a sense of their distinctiveness. The women especially have become aware that the social construction of gender roles in Saudi Arabia distinguishes them from other Arab women and radically divides them from Europeans and Americans. Gender, in Saudi Arabia, is thus a positive and negative force in identity construction for both men and women. For example, Dania (24), from Jeddah, believes that positive 'male–female encounters prior to marriage could take place *bidun ghalat* (without sinning)'. But because of Saudi society these meetings can only happen abroad, 'because in Saudi Arabia there are no public places for men and women to meet. ... In Saudi Arabia a woman's reputation is more at stake.'

Maha says that she finds studying in a foreign country a big effort. However, it is necessary because Saudi women have regressed. 'We must study so that we can influence others.' Maha's ambition is to succeed in her studies. She believes that she must satisfy herself by specializing in a career, keeping a balance between cultural demands and her own needs. Maha is a *muhajjaba* and this gives her a stronger moral base to question or criticize women's position. Her language expresses the Muslim feminist approach, but whether conservative or modernist, the majority of activists appear to be stretching the limits of Saudi gender boundaries.

6 Religion: reviving Islamic identity

Within non-democratic developing countries empirical evidence of the existence of civil society, however defined, is often hard to uncover. Where the government seeks to coopt and control all areas of society, to minimize opposition to its rule, it is often only religious organizations that retain enough autonomy or cohesion to shelter the vestiges of civil society. So in the Middle East in general, it is often easier to find examples of opposition elements or sentiment around religious organizations because they offer shelter to or promote independent social groupings in the face of state repression. This can lead to groups with a religious heritage or ideology dominating the political arena when resentment against the government increases or if controls are relaxed.

The world-view offered by Islam remains the fundamental frame of reference for the personal and collective identity of all Saudi Arabians. This is especially the case with those who have benefited least from and are most traumatized by the Western style of modernization. Religious symbols remain the main way left open to the mass of the population today to explain and control modernity, which could otherwise be perceived as presenting an all-powerful and devastating force operating in a senseless fashion. Islamic discourse at a cultural level is an instrument with which to regain identity and assimilate a kind of modernity that would otherwise be alienating. At a political level, it can offer a language which combines a criticism of the regime with pledges of loyalty.

Those with more radical and even revolutionary aims can use Islamist ideology as a platform for their demands and an instrument for the organization of opposition to the regime they perceive as corrupt and inefficient. The Islamist discourse proposes an organic and self-sufficient view of the world and therefore a solid point of reference for collective and individual identity. By deploying symbolism crucial to the self-identity of the population, the Islamists may actually aim to become the coherent voice of opposition and a channel for socio-economic interests marginalized or ignored by the state.

Since the 1980s there has been an increase in the public expression of 'piety' in Saudi Arabia. This was due to the 1979 Islamic revolution in neighbouring Iran as well as the Russian invasion of Afghanistan. After the 1990–91 Gulf war, '... Islam has become, once again, a two-edged political instrument – as the Kingdom's primary medium of self-legitimation, and as the main venue of protest for opposition elements.'[1] What revived Islam as the political vehicle for opposition was the negative but material conception of the state. The state, it was claimed, became rich but did not deal adequately with its wealth or distribute it equitably. The perceived corruption and mismanagement of wealth as well as inequality of the distribution of welfare was the key to the Islamist critique and gave rise to calls for 'Islamic justice'. There was also a perceived need by the Islamist opposition for the state to become more Islamic in order to protect the values of the individual and the *umma* (Islamic nation). In the Saudi *salafi* way of thinking this is a localized *umma* upholding Saudi national concerns.

Islam is one of the core values – if not *the* core value – at the heart of the identity of the new generation across Saudi Arabia. Different forms or components of identity are expressed relative to the social context, as seen in the previous chapter; hence, while family belonging is a pervasive form, young people are going through redefinitions of the hierarchy and gender relations, and Islam appears to be the dominant building block of Saudi identity. Amina (18) is representative of this general view: 'In Saudi Arabia you can learn control and respect. You also learn compassion for Muslims. I learn here about religion. I couldn't have learnt it anywhere else. The angle from which to look at Islam is different [from that of non-Saudis] but ultimately the core belief never changes.'

All the changes that have taken place during the lives of the last three generations of Saudi Arabians have given rise to profound questioning that has been mediated through the certainties of religion. The young

---

[1] R. Hrair Dekmejian, 'The Rise of Political Islamism in Saudi Arabia', *Middle East Journal*, Vol. 48, No. 4, Autumn 1994, p. 627.

people of the Kingdom are faced with changing realities at the national, regional and global level. In these unsettling times, Islam appears to offer them a sense of security and identity; they rely on it to represent coherence and a continuous link back to the certainties of their grandparents' generation, as well as an apparently stable vantage point from which they can judge the external world.

All the young people interviewed expressed a desire for Saudi Arabia to remain a Muslim society ruled by an overtly Muslim state. But this opinion is far more heterogeneous than it at first appears. The role Islam will play in the future of Saudi Arabia and the form it will take are deeply contested. On the basis of the interviews conducted, I have identified three broad approaches among the new generation to the religion that plays such a crucial part in their identities. These groups fluctuate according to the issues that are being considered, but based on self-definition they range from the 'liberal modernists' to the 'traditionalists' to the 'conservative' *salafis*, with the 'radical' *salafis* making up the mobilized and alienated fringe.

The group identified as 'liberal modernists' have a diffuse sense of religious belonging but actively and optimistically engage with what they see as the modernizing secular culture of the West. This has left their formal religious observance at a minimum. Taking on the motifs of secular politics, they put their faith in the rationality of the individual. From this perspective, the regime of the Al-Saud and the Al Shaykh will have limited problems with their legitimacy as long as they govern with minimum interference and maximum efficiency. For this group it is crucial that Saudi Arabia must be allowed to progress and develop towards a market economy keeping up with the demands of the integrated global economy. The modernists are defined by their pragmatism. Their main concern is to see social and economic progress. The state, they hope, will gradually move to decrease its role in the economic and especially the moral lives of the population. Islam, for this group, is still key to their self-definition, but it is an Islam that allows individual choice as to how best to be a good Muslim and an Islam that does not clash with the benefits of progress. They believe that women should be allowed to develop careers, albeit within a traditional framework that preserves their honour and gives priority to raising children. For this group, although religion and tradition are less important than for others, a constant balancing act is needed between the new and potentially unsettling and the old and certain.

The 'traditionalists', who represent the majority of those interviewed, and indeed most probably the majority of ordinary Saudi Arabians, are concerned with maintaining a coherent and constant Islamic identity and protecting the values they regard as crucial to it. They worry about and are threatened by the effects of Westernization, especially satellite television and the increased commercialization of Saudi society. They believe that some separation of gender is crucial to maintain moral probity. The traditionalists believe in obedience to Islamic principles as laid down by the religious establishment and political obedience to the rule of Al-Saud. The *uli al-amr* (those with authority) must be obeyed. Their view of Islam is fused with the vision of the Saudi nation that is united behind the governing elite. For the traditionalists, the world beyond the borders of the Kingdom, especially the Western world, harbours potential but very real dangers. Modernization, though unavoidable and necessary, must be mediated through the already known, through the cultural certainties of Islam.

The conservative *salafis* also attach nationalistic feelings to their Islamic beliefs and recognize the authority of the religious establishment. However, they think that they are *uli al-amr* and have the 'right' to advise Saudi society to remain on the true path. This is especially the case for the conservative *salafis* who believe strongly in the concept of the *umma*. They would like to see a distinctive Saudi *wahhabi* society, distinguished by the application of local tribal values, that would shape everyone's moral, social and political behaviour. The conservative *salafis* believe, for example, that although women work and appear in public in other Muslim countries, this should not be tolerated in the Saudi context. Despite their vocal adherence to an Islamist ideology, those identified in interviews as conservative *salafis* did not express the desire for serious political change and share with the majority of the new generation a 'can't do' attitude. What cannot be done is anything that would involve organized collective political dissent or an overt challenge to the state. The distinctive element in their way of thinking is the call for civil reform within the Islamic system. They also have a profound perception of the cultural contradictions produced by unrestricted access to 'modernity' and the problems this brings.

The radical *salafis* believe that there is a crisis of legitimacy at the heart of the political system under the Al-Saud. The decline in the moral probity of the governing elite has driven a general national degeneration and reduced economic efficiency. This sense of dire pessimism finds a focus in worries about demographic growth which has not been accompanied by adequate economic development. The radical *salafis* are also the only group openly and actively to reject the regime, claiming that they are organizing a mass challenge to the Al-Saud regime's legitimacy and hence its longevity. The radical *salafis* perceive that the economic and social problems faced by the country result from deviance from the true Islamic path embodied in the *shari'a*. All social achievements will become realizable once respect for the *shari'a* has been restored. For them the *salafi* interpretation of Islam remains the only way left open for Saudis today to control modernity and safely deploy the technological advances available from outside the Kingdom. This view finds particular resonance among members of the new middle class who have benefited least from the welfare system and who are unemployed. They express a clear and coherent fear of the Western-style modernization they see unfolding in Saudi Arabia and the ambiguity of the authorities' response to its negative consequences. This group of Saudi youth who find solace in Islamic ideology want to see not only an Islamic state but also one with a radically different approach from that of the present regime. Hence, this mode of thought is explicitly directed towards political action. For them, a society of good Muslims can only be achieved in a state purged of Western-inspired decadence and corruption. The envisaged state has to be run by a government that is truly Islamic.

A range of opinions surfaced in the interviews about the United States that appear at best ambivalent and at worst actively hostile. The more conservative and radical *salafis* tend to have the strongest animosity towards Americans, whom they depict as the political and economic occupying force of Saudi Arabia. The United States is seen in this respect as an old-style colonial power with the Al-Saud acting as morally and politically weak collaborators, supported by a coopted and thus compromised religious establishment. They cite the second Gulf war as a key example of this trend, with the late bin Baz, the then grand Mufti of the country, issuing a *fatwa* (religious edict) providing what they consider to be religious cover for unacceptable political relations with non-believers.[2] It is noteworthy that those who call for thorough reform of political and social institutions are few in number and marginalized, while the traditionalists and conservatives who tend towards a coherent but limited compromise represent the norm.

Very little stress was placed by any of the interviewees on the spiritual dimension of religion. This is especially the case for the overtly religious and radical *salafis*. The language of practical and rational problem-solving was deployed time and again to explain and tackle the sins of corruption and the inadequacies of governmental institutions. This may be explained by the fact that the dominant *salafi wahhabi* Islam of the state does not allow for the ritualistic spiritual expression that characterizes regional Islamic variations, both in the Hijazi Sufi[3] tradition and in Shi'a Islamic practice.[4] But despite widespread criticism of the state's handling of Islam, there was very little evidence of an organized or widespread expression of regional Islamic differences. In practice there are some exceptions to the trend this denotes, notably the ceremony of *ashura* (the Shi'a annual mourning for the death of Hussein) and the Hijazi celebration of the *mawlid* (the ceremony of the birth of the Prophet).[5] These ceremonies are not approved of by the religious establishment but have an increasing following among those who religiously and geographically believe themselves to be marginalized from a specifically *wahhabi* and Saudi establishment. Among those interviewed the general absence of references to regional Islamic differences can be explained by the fact that all of the new generation have been brought up

[2] The *fatwa* issued in 1990 agreeing to seek help from what are described in all *wahhabi* teaching as 'infidels' was justified on grounds of necessity. See Mustafa Alani and Andrew Rathmell, 'Special Report', *Jane's Intelligence Review*, No. 2, 1996, p. 16.

[3] Sufism is part orthodox Islam, sharing a belief in the *shari'a*, and part mysticism, believing that the truth about God has not been revealed but continues to lie hidden. Although there are different *tariqah* (methods of prayer) for moving through the different stages (*magamat*) on the way to God, all Sufis hold it is possible to attain a 'purity of vision' of God through various meditative or trance inducing practices. Chanting, music and dance, contemplating the soul and meditation are all used.

[4] The Saudi Shi'a number between 250,000 and 400,000 and are mainly located in the cities of Qatif, Hufuf, Sayhat and Al-Hasa in the eastern province. According to *wahhabis*, the Shi'a are condemned as *ahl al-bid'a* (innovators). But since 1980 the Saudi authorities have gone out of their way to 'manage' the Shi'a opposition in the eastern province. In addition to providing generous inflows of financial support several members of the royal family have visited Shi'a dignitaries. See J. Kechichian, 'Islamic Revivalism and Change in Saudi Arabia', p. 5.

[5] The date of the Prophet's birth is believed to be on Monday (the night of the Tuesday) the 12th of Rabi al-Awwal. See Nico Kapstein, 'Materials for the History of the Prophet Muhammad's Birthday Celebration in Mecca', *Der Islam*, Vol. 69, No. 2, 1992.

under a highly centralized and uniform Islam controlled by the ruling elite.

But the lack of space within Saudi society for open display of religious spirituality has given rise to other forms of non-institutionalized belief. During the interviews, a number of young people made explicit reference to *'amal* (witchcraft) and *hasad* ('the evil eye') as phenomena that they have witnessed negatively affecting people around them. These concepts are not new in traditional Gulf societies and were a key part of their grandparents' beliefs. There appears to be a resurgence in such beliefs today caused by the uncertainties and fears that permeate the lives of the young. Traditionally, whenever things went wrong a number of possible explanations were given, both rational and non-rational, seen and unseen. Unforeseen or uncontrollable events are attributed principally to witchcraft and other evil spirits. The legitimacy of such beliefs is grounded in Islamic thought because they are mentioned in the Quran.[6] However, excessive reference to these 'superstitions' and measures taken to counteract evil are not accepted by the religious authorities. Some 'superstitious practices', along with witchcraft, are legally punishable. The only officially acceptable defence against these practices is the reciting of the relevant verses from the Quran. Nevertheless, the youth encounter 'the evil eye' and other beliefs in their everyday life. According to Hind, not all students enrol for a second year at medical school: 'My friend who was so keen to become a medical doctor suddenly got frightened, had a block caused by *hasad* and dropped out from university.' When a friend or a colleague fails to attend exams or when the marriage of a family member breaks up, *'amal* is feared. They find reaffirmation of such beliefs from sermons at certain mosques that warn against the dangers of witchcraft. Hani (18) asked his mother to remove all family photographs from the living room for fear that they would become objects of witchcraft. He affirmed his belief by referring to a particular speech of an imam at the mosque warning of the dangers of photography in terms of both indecent exposure and the potential for witchcraft. On the whole, the *sheitan* (the devil) remains a large, if unseen, force in young people's everyday life, symbolizing a sense of pessimism and lack of control over the circumstances they find themselves in.

---

[6] Quran, *Surat al-Falaq* (The Dawn), No. 113, verse 5.

Islam and the state in Saudi Arabia

Since the unification of the country in 1932 the political power of government has been so closely entwined with that of the *wahhabi* elite that they serve to legitimize each other. The nature of Saudi Arabia's politico-religious alliance makes it unique in the Islamic and Arab world. The country is theoretically governed according to 'God's law', and the ruler is the executor entrusted with applying 'God's law'. Al-Rasheed has argued that the Saudi state has striven to marginalize the role of the religious authorities in the life of everyday Saudi Arabians to little more than 'educating the masses in matters relating to *fiqh*, Islamic jurisprudence, such as prayers and ablutions'.[7]

The nature of this alliance between the secular political power of the state and the religious power of *wahhabi* Islam has given rise to problems as well as strengthening the governing elite. The crucial problems of the limits of secular authority and the scope and nature of religious authority have been a constant source of tension between the political establishment and those active within and around religious institutions. This ambiguity has led to criticisms of the elite for both its politico-economic and its socio-religious policies: 'The monarchy was vulnerable precisely because some of the Islamist attacks reflected the grass-roots complaints of many Saudis about the prevailing shortcomings of the kingdom's socio-political life.'[8]

Unsurprisingly the extent and nature of the state's role in enforcing religious standards has been the focus of much debate and contestation among the new generation, as was noted in Chapter 2. Layla (15) epitomizes the clash of attitudes about the duality of state authority in her belief that when the state acts as the guardian of Islam it should not be as rigid as it is at present and, more importantly, it should certainly not be inconsistent. Although she does not conclude that the state should not be the guardian of Islam, her education and exposure abroad have led her to begin to develop a critical view of the role of the state in guarding religious observance. This, combined with a heightened political consciousness, means that she has placed the blame for the inconsistencies in

[7] Madawi Al-Rasheed, 'Saudi Arabia's Islamic Opposition', *Current History*, January 1996, p. 21.
[8] R. Hrair Dekmejian, 'The Rise of Political Islamism in Saudi Arabia', p. 638.

application on the extensive role of guardian that the state took up in the first place.

Ghalib (17) also considers that it is the state's role to impose Islamic values, but not to the extent of hindering people's freedoms. Ghalib thinks that 'there is a clash between people's freedom and imposing strict Islamic values'. He has begun to articulate the tensions between an individualistic notion of human rights and rationality and the state's role as ultimate guardian of morality. Ultimately, he thinks, the state's role should be minimized to being the final guarantor of morality and Islam; it should not be the active imposer of a greater morality on its population.

Naif (23), on the other hand, expresses the mainstream, conservative support of the status quo. In his opinion, it is the state's role to impose and guard Islamic values. Interestingly, however, he still has problems with the way the state has carried out its duties. 'We have done the job badly,' he laments. Like all the members of the new generation interviewed, he does not believe that Saudi Arabia can do without Islam, but he is highly critical of the interpretations of Islam that the state currently uses. Such practices as gender segregation, in his opinion, are not Islamic; thus there needs to be a redefinition of the state's view. He believes that tradition and continuity gives an 'Islamic theological nucleus' to society. But it is interesting that he goes on to limit its application by emphatically declaring that social limitations have become part of what is provided by tradition. As for the problems that modernity have brought to Saudi Arabia, he classifies the main debate as revolving around what is Islamic versus non-Islamic. But he is reluctant to take a definite stance on such a controversial issue: 'In this debate I am not sure where I stand.'

Ahmed (21) represents the minority view. He does not believe that it is the state's role to impose or guard Islamic values at all. For Ahmed religion is a personal matter between the individual and his God. He has a very individualistic view and consciously labels himself as a modernist. This does not mean that he altogether rejects an Islamic basis to society; on the contrary, he sees it as a good thing, but crucially he feels it should be chosen by free-thinking autonomous individuals.

The public face of Islamic guardianship is the *mutaw'a* (the religious police), who take it upon themselves to root out anti-Islamic or sinful practices. The influence and visibility of the *mutaw'a* can be taken as an indicator of how much the government is playing to the conservative trend within Saudi society in attempting to shore up its base of support. The government is perceived by both modern and traditional types as giving extra power to the *mutaw'a* to underline its Islamic credentials. Among the members of the new generation, the *mutaw'a* employees of *al-hay'a* ('The Committee' for the propagation of good and the forbidding of evil) represent not only the most visible guardians of Islam but also the most restrictive public force that can place limits on their life. Attitudes towards the *mutaw'a* and *al-hay'a*, therefore, become a key indicator of more general views about the state's role both as guardian of Islam and in restricting personal conduct, development and freedom.

Nouf (23), for example, believes that 'Saudi Arabia is very closed'. She cites *al-hay'a* as partially responsible for this: '*al-hay'a* sometimes over-restrict people's movement and behaviour when in public.' But her criticism of their role is limited. She thinks that the government must continue to pay them respect because '*al-hay'a* have showed more restraint in their approach'. The apparent contradiction in her view is partially explained by her statement that she values Islam and especially *salafi*. 'We should maintain the traditional segregation of the sexes because of the general conservative Islamic trends that still exist in society.' This young princess is keen to maintain the religious outlook of society and the power of the Al-Saud, her family. She sees the religious underpinning of the Al-Saud's legitimacy as crucial to this and *al-hay'a* as a key instrument for its continuation. At a different level, Haifa (15) sees the 'protective' role of the *mutaw'a*. According to her, 'they are good for society and for Saudi morals and traditions'. To this young *muhajjaba* the *mutaw'a* represent control and continuity.

By contrast, Ghazi (15), a Shi'a from the eastern province, sees *al-hay'a* as an uncontrolled nuisance. He is against the strict behaviour that 'they and their *mutaw'a* impose. The government should control them'. He goes on to argue that 'I am not rejecting *al-hay'a*' [but] they must be reformed and made accountable'. Ghazi does not then blame the government for what he sees as the excesses of *al-hay'a's* behaviour, but he does see the government as responsible for controlling them. For Ghazi, the government has a role in regulating religious observance, but that role and the role of *al-hay'a* should be placed within strict limits that ultimately respect the individual's ability to choose how she or he worships.

Dana (15), who, as noted in Chapter 2, believes that 'religious extremism is bad and the *mutaw'a* are bad for society', perceives the rules governing Islamic conduct to be identical with those that the *mutaw'a* seek to enforce. Hence she identifies Islam in Saudi Arabia with the *mutaw'a*, whom she does not approve of because they clash with 'modern developments' that she sees as positive. Sara (15) also believes that the *mutaw'a* are excessive in their religious approach and does not like their behaviour. Like Dana, she sees herself as a modernist and she identifies the Islam of the Saudi state with the repression of the *mutaw'a*.

Dunya (15) develops this argument to state explicitly that the values of her generation should become less religious/extremist. For her this would mean less allowance for *al-hay'a*, 'who hit people', for example women who are not veiled properly in the market-place. Dunya believes that modernity is open-mindedness. She does not reject Islamic values, but regards *al-hay'a* as an impediment to change. All three of these fifteen-year-olds view the prohibitions placed on women as a hindrance inappropriately applied to Saudi society in the name of religion.

The 'liberal modernists'

The idea that state-imposed Islam is somehow responsible for holding back Saudi Arabia is a view shared by both the self-styled 'modernists' and the 'conservative' *salafis*. Both see the state's role as wrong, but reform has radically different meanings for the two groups.

Sami links what he sees as the constraints of Islamic interpretations to specific Saudi traditions: 'We are limited by tribal Islamic traditions. *Al-taqalid ma tismah* – traditions do not permit.' For Faiz (16) it is the interpretation of Islam that is the problem: 'In Saudi Arabia religion is not applied correctly and therefore it is an obstacle to progress.' For him, as for other liberals, observance of most rules should be a matter of personal choice. For example, he thinks the wearing of the veil is a matter for each individual, since it has not been specified in the Quran. Although Faiz's ideas are self-consciously 'modernist', he still wants to adhere to Islam. However, he considers that the Islam of the authorities must be modified. The young 'liberal modernists' perceive their position to be gradualist in nature. Reforms must be carried out but they have to take place from within the Islamic framework, not outside it.

The 'traditionalists' and the 'conservative' salafis

By far the largest group of those interviewed, and probably the most representative group of Saudi society as a whole, are those who could be labelled 'conservative' and who conceive of themselves as 'traditionalists'. They represent the solid base of support that backs the regime as a whole and its day-to-day policies. To portray these young people as resistant to change or unaware of the wider world beyond the boundaries of their country would be wrong. For example, Hadi (23) regularly uses the Internet and is very positive about its benefits. But like the majority of the conservatives questioned, he wants to limit access to the full forces of globalization, especially the cultural effects. According to him, anything that overtly breaks Islamic law should be forbidden. Access to the Internet, for example, should be selective: 'It should not access things that contradict the Islamic religion.' He goes on to argue that Saudi traditions should be maintained, including gender segregation and the veil. 'A lot of progress has been achieved in Saudi Arabia, but there should be boundaries.' Hadi is a good example of the conservative outlook common in the Kingdom. His central concern is the waves of modernity he sees sweeping over the Gulf region. These clash with the familiar world of tradition, putting morality and stability at risk. He does not wish to see more change, especially if it threatens his religion.

Abdul Wahid (24), like Hadi, puts his faith for stability and a positive future in 'traditions' which he unthinkingly equates with the state's interpretation of Islam. When questioned further on which specific traditions are positive he says simply that 'most Saudi traditions are good for society' and that 'we should maintain gender segregation in educational and professional spheres as well as the veil'. But Abdul Wahid also expresses a strong belief in the flexibility of Islam. This will continue to allow Muslims to adapt technology to benefit and strengthen Islamic society. He is not totally uncritical of the Saudi state, arguing that a more Islamic application of progress would result in greater quality of access to its benefits and that this should be sorted out by the authorities.

Daghas (23) thinks that social values should be maintained but seems to have a more detailed idea than Abdul Wahid of what these traditions are. The best are 'family solidarity and generosity'. However, he overtly distinguishes these from negative traditions such as 'the tribal prejudice, which is not good and does not always comply with religion'. So Daghas, although believing in the importance of Islamic doctrine for all Saudis, distinguishes this from more secular traditions such as family and tribal solidarity. This distinction allows him assess critically the benefits of each of these traditions without criticizing what he sees as the central tenets of Islam.

Issam (21), like many of his contemporaries, defines modernity simply as the West. 'We must take the best that is applicable to our culture and keep away from what contradicts our religion. I would use any technological thing that does not contradict my religion.' When asked about the position of satellite television he was hesitant, but then declared that 'there are good and bad programmes and aspects to it'. Like many of the new generation, Issam sees the forces of modernity and 'the West' as inevitable. The priority then becomes judging what can benefit Saudi society and what must be excluded to protect Islam. He looks up to and trusts the state to carry out this task.

Abdul Wahid has been socialized to make sure that his behaviour does not venture outside the boundaries of what he has been taught to consider good Islamic behaviour. All that is 'Islamic' is good and all that is not must be avoided. He believes, therefore, that it is permissible for a man to see his future wife before marriage, but only in the presence of her family. This, he says, 'is Islamic'. Abdul Karim (23) has similar views. He believes in polygamous marriage: 'It is what Allah permits man.' These ideas spring from his direct family experience, as Abdul Karim does not wish the world of his father (who had more than one wife) and of his grandfather to change. He believes this continuity will only be possible through strict adherence to Islam. The ultimate example of Islam overriding modernity, in his mind, is the right of a Saudi man to have more than one wife and hence many children, conserving in this way the world of family and the nation.

The 'radicals'

In contrast to the views of the 'traditionalists', the 'radical' Islamists of the new generation interviewed hold the state responsible for what they see as the degeneration of Saudi society under the Western and modernist onslaught. But interestingly, although traditional Islamic theology pays only marginal attention to the state and its role, these modern Islamists have identified the Saudi state as both the problem and the solution. The state has to be captured and the present regime thrown out. Government institutions can then be transformed to become the instruments for guaranteeing a truly Islamic society and protecting the population from Western corruption.

This new brand of Islamic radicals is itself a product of state-driven development in education and employment. Unlike Juhayman al-Utaybi's al-Ikhwan group which seized the Grand Mosque in November 1979, these radicals are predominantly urban, university-educated sons of the new middle classes who have earned their living in the state bureaucracy. The threat they pose for the authorities is more insidious and harder to combat. The are well organized and have mastered the language of both Islam and of modern notions of rational government and liberal equality. This they deploy to rally those alienated by both state inefficiencies and the effects of globalization. As Dekmejian observes, 'the new Islamists' higher level of political discourse is reflected in their cassettes and memoranda when compared with the Ikhwan's less sophisticated ideology as seen in Juhayman bin al-Sayf al-'Utaybi, Saba' Rasa'il (Seven Letters) ...'.[9] Thus education and technological advancements have helped the new Islamists in their agenda.

But this new movement, because of its strict adherence to *wahhabi* Islam, remains sectarian in nature and based primarily in the Nejd. These new *salafis* have moulded a potent Islamic ideology that manages to criticize both the Saudi state and alien forces of instability and injustice. Abdul Aziz (30) is a good example. He is deeply critical of the way in which the state handles Islamic values. He emphasizes the Islamic identity of Saudi Arabia, its people and its culture. However, he is critical of the fact that the 'sultan' (he does not use the word 'king', because that is God's position) interferes in some of the minute details affecting the lives of his 'subjects'. There is very little room for manoeuvre; everything is imposed on the people, even those details not relating to religious practice. People should be allowed freedom of expression. This is their legitimate Islamic right. People should be allowed to choose and discriminate between what is really Islamic and what is deviant.

Abdul Aziz has subconsciously combined the language of Islamist opposition with a discourse on individual rights to be free of a powerful state. This mode of thought is much more common in the industrialized West and owes its popularity to the neo-classical economic trends of the 1980s. It is the hybrid nature of this political discourse that has made it appealing to those seeking explanations for a rapidly changing world.

Although a Sunni, Abdul Aziz shows a similarly diverse taste in influences:

The Islamic revolution in Iran is a unique experiment, one that has succeeded in many aspects, despite the fact that its road was thorny. Khomeini is to be praised by Muslims for his ideas, for he had addressed many concerns of the Iranian youth. We have yet to go through these reforms.

Unsurprisingly, he also takes heart from Afghanistan, where, he says,

the Taliban movement has been portrayed wrongly in the media, especially the Western media who are waging a campaign of distortion and lies against this Islamic movement. The media are doing their best to prevent the establishment of an Islamic system there.

Abdul Aziz suspects that the Taliban are not as bad as they are portrayed, and as a Sunni he relates more to them than to the Iranian Shi'a Muslims. His dislike of the United States is stronger and more coherent than among the majority of the new generation interviewed. 'The United States is doing its best to ruin our country. It is doing its best to rule us. We have almost no right or say in what is happening; they are trying their best to corrupt our Islamic identity.' But Abdul Aziz spent one year living in the United Kingdom, and his dislike of modernity embraces the majority of Western countries. He talked about what he perceived as a 'war' between the West and Islam and expressed admiration for Osama bin Laden's courage in his long fight against corruption and the United States. He concluded his remarks on religion by declaring that 'without religion we have no pride; only with religion can we have pride. Before the prophet Muhammad we were *juhalla* (ignorant) and now we must fight to maintain the true Islam of our forbears.'

Hamad (29), like the majority of those interviewed, classifies himself first and foremost as a Muslim. But he shares a radical *salafi* stance with Abdul Aziz, especially with regard to the United States:

> As for the Americans, the least I can say about them is that they are thieves who are stealing our money, money that we need for our own people, and this is the biggest puzzle – how are they allowed to rob us like this? What is our relationship with the Americans? We went to ask the Princes, who have nothing to say. We are a colonized country, colonized by America.

Unlike Abdul Aziz, Hamad sees the state's role as much more domin-ant in ensuring the morality of society. He asserted that it was the state's role to impose Islamic values but clarified that 'it must be in ways pleasant to the people, in compliance with their needs'. The problem with the present government was that 'it selects from Islam what it wants for its own purpose, for its own legitimacy. This is the problem, in its political use of Islam.' Hamad sees himself as an Islamist, criticizing corruption, especially *rashwa* (bribery). He speaks the language of the Committee for Defence of Legitimate Rights (CDLR), with which he sympathizes and is in close contact.

Conclusion

Islam, for all these young people, is key to their self-perception. It remains the main ideational force that gives coherence to their world. All those interviewed are aware of the wide-ranging changes that have swept through Saudi Arabia during their lifetime. It is Islam and 'tradition' that help them to put these changes into perspective. Islamic discourse is central to their self-understanding and is readily available to those who wish to contest the status quo and undermine the Al-Saud's legitimacy. Although the radical Islamists are in a small minority, their language, identifying corruption and demonizing the West, finds an echo among many of the new generation. As the state's ability to underwrite social stability with oil wealth declines, the voice of Islamic opposition could well find more supporters.

7 The new generation and the future: rethinking Saudi Arabia

A rapid transformation in all aspects of life has been the norm for three generations of Saudis since the founding of the contemporary Kingdom. What distinguishes the circumstances of members of the new generation is the sheer pressure of numbers in a contracting economy, which is undermining the perceived certainties of their parents and grandparents. Their numbers alone also make them a major political and economic constituency in the Gulf area at the turn of the century. Their views, hopes and fears and, crucially, their capacity or inclination for collective action will be a major determinant of stability not just in Saudi Arabia but in the whole region.

In a country that is relatively closed, where public opinion is difficult to evaluate or measure, the thoughts and behaviour of this baby-boom generation have become the object of much ill-informed speculation among those who study the Kingdom from the outside. The lack of substantive information about the new generation is all the more worrying in the light of evidence that the nation built by King Abdul Aziz Al-Saud in the early 1930s and later developed and expanded by King Faisal in the early 1970s is now showing signs of strain. The Kingdom successfully weathered the political storms of the 1950s, 1960s and 1970s, but the future will depend on how Saudi youngsters see themselves and on their capacity to manage change.

It is against this background that I have spent the last two years interviewing young people between the ages of 15 and 30 from all sections of society, focusing on members of the new middle class. My aim has been to reveal how today's youth perceive and describe their own immediate circumstances and how they see themselves in relation to the new realities of the changing and globalizing world. As the interviews progressed the theme of identity came increasingly to dominate and permeate the entire study. Individual members of the new generation have identities which are in the process of redefinition and possibly transformation.

Because identity is a dynamic phenomenon, in both a social and a political context, the economic and cultural changes that Saudi Arabia continues to undergo have generated new expressions of individual identity. While economic change and the pressures of globalization have resulted in the expansion of the horizons of the new generation, at the same time they have undermined the stability of its familiar world. Among the building blocks of identity available to today's youth are residual customs and traditions together with new notions of belonging at the regional, national and global levels. Their Islamic and Arab heritage are central influences. In addition, more specific sub-national, regional and tribal roots jostle with professional, educational and now even unemployed identities. The new generation is in the process of developing its own hybrid identity that springs directly from its peculiar set of circumstances.

As the study has highlighted, Saudi youth continue to compare their reality with that of their parents and with the values their parents espouse for them. Against this background, the technological results of globalization are widely available, ranging from mobile phones and the Internet to videos of the latest Hollywood films, Western music, satellite television and the other consumer accessories of youth culture. But within this playground of competing influences there has developed a detectable standard of behaviour across Saudi Arabia that is distinctive and powerful. The process of national socialization, primarily achieved through a unified educational system and the mass media, has cut across regions, tribes, and even religion. The common acceptance of a relatively uniform set of norms is the product of a distinctively Saudi experience. It places very real restrictions on what the new generation can and cannot do. For those I interviewed this is a source of both reassurance and frustration.

The key theme to emerge in all the interviews I conducted was the clash between a national, rigorous socialization and the uncertainties and promises stemming from wider access to different cultural influences. The majority of these young people recognize the nature and extent of the changes that they and their generation face. In their encounter with uncertainty most prove able to draw on three constants as a source of stability: the family, Islam and the nation. This book has attempted to chart the role these three strands have played in the identities, lives and futures of the new generation. The mix is dynamic and each individual is engaged in developing his or her own balance between tradition and modernity.

The interviews reveal a predictable spectrum of views ranging from traditional conservatism to extreme consumerism. In the discussion of national identity, interviewees emerge on a spectrum ranging from passive resignation to rebellious activism. Attitudes towards economic decline range from the fatalist to the realist, with the latter representing the majority and a small minority emerging as alienated activists. The influence of religion on identity construction appears to be the most constant theme across the board. The vast majority of the new generation perceive Islam as the stable and unchallenged base of their identity and the guideline for everyday life. There were certainly differences in how the interviewees saw the principles and role of Islam in society, public and private life, but there was little evidence to suggest any process of overt secularization. Uncertainty and increased exposure to a wider range of influences has, if anything, brought home the central role Islam plays in delivering a stable base from which to interact with a changing world.

The strict boundaries defined by gender identity, however, are no longer unchallenged. Gender roles put under pressure in previous generations by economic change are now being actively questioned by those young women who want to utilize the benefits of the modern education system to which they have had access. At one end of the spectrum of views of young men and women concerning gender segregation and family responsibility are those who subscribe to what they see as the roles given to them by tradition and society. This position imputes respect for the patriarchal family, with women continuing their role in the private sphere of the family and home. But the majority reveal discomfort with such a rigid conception of gender roles. These members of the new generation are in search of a compromise between their personal expectations and the demands of family and society. They are aware of and sympathetic to the increasing demands for women to have a larger role in the workplace. Finally, at the other end of the spectrum there is a minority of feminists.

Overall the majority of those interviewed may be seen as pragmatists. They share a diffuse sense of unease and dissatisfaction but seek a gradualist approach to solving the problems they have identified in Saudi society. These negative views have a target, and it is the Saudi state. All those interviewed share a sense of nationality. But this collective identity has been deployed against the perceived shortcomings of the state. This is in no way a precursor to a rebellious or activist movement, but it does show a general if incoherent dissatisfaction with the state and the services it deploys.

Abdul Rahman, Muna and Muhammad: examples of the new generation

Members of the new generation have honoured me with their stories. Their thoughts portray the complexity of responding to the ambiguous and dynamic character of a globalized economic system. In an attempt to encapsulate the range of opinions I encountered over two years of interviews, I have constructed three composite representatives of Saudi youth. This device will allow me to convey more graphically the complex mix of views that came out in the interviews across a range of subjects without endangering the anonymity of those interviewed. Abdul Rahman, Muna and Muhammad represent an amalgamation of the spectrum of experiences and opinions I encountered. I have deliberately constructed them to depict contrasting as well as common responses found among the real interviewees to the challenges they all face.

Abdul Rahman's story

My name is Abdul Rahman. I was born in 1974. I come from Sakaka, the capital of al-Jawf, a region that lies to the north of Saudi Arabia, near the border with Jordan.

My family owns a farm in Sakaka where they grow oranges and lemons renowned for their flavour and taste. My father's name is Abdul Karim, and that of my mother is Hasnaa'. Unlike many parents of my generation, mine do not actually come from the same town. My mother comes originally from a village to the west of Sakaka, called al-Qaryat. I know al-Qaryat very well, as I go there to visit my maternal uncles and cousins. With Allah's blessings my maternal and paternal family, although not from the same lineage, are well suited to each other.

I am the seventh of eight children. The eldest is my brother 'Adel, who works as a tradesman on the Saudi–Jordanian border. He has dual nationality, Jordanian and Saudi. This, I believe, is not unusual in our part of the world.

I completed both my primary and secondary education at the local school in Sakaka. Life in Sakaka was hardly what one would call exciting, but we felt secure as we grew up, unaware of the complexities and problems that lay ahead. At the time I hardly knew that there was anything more to life than my experiences in my birthplace. Life revolved around our farm, my school, gatherings after school until sunset and of course the mosque. The outside world seemed to me too big and too distant to hold any interest or make any impact on my life. I was just not bothered at all by what happened in the outside world; as far as I was concerned, I could not see how events outside Sakaka – even those occurring within Saudi Arabia's borders – could affect me or my family. Or so I happily believed.

I think it was not until the age of sixteen that I started realizing how the 'outside world' could have an impact upon me; in fact, what I considered to be the outside world was suddenly transported to our doorsteps. That which was foreign, alien and un-Islamic was all of a sudden right in our midst, and there was very little that we could do about it – at least those of us living in Sakaka. Iraq's invasion of Kuwait and the ensuing Gulf War was a time of immense change and confusion. For the first time in my life, and like all the other children at school, I was gripped by the pictures that were constantly being transmitted onto our television screens. For the first time in my life, I saw Israel – that all-too-powerful country of Zionists, the enemies of Muslims – being bombed by Saddam Hussein. It was a most fascinating event. I had always heard the Arabs go on and on about Israel and the injustices it had done to others, but this was the first time someone was doing something about it, and we in Sakaka were geographically the nearest to all these events.

But while Saddam's missile attacks on Israel were a source of fascination for all of us in Sakaka, there was another aspect of the war that we found deeply disturbing and confusing. Television stations such as Jordan TV were transmitting pictures of demonstrations across the Arab and Islamic worlds in support of Iraq's annexation of Kuwait and protesting about the war effort against Iraq. Since there was hardly any news of this on Saudi state television, not even announcements about the invasion, we realized that there was heavy censorship of news, and we lost trust in the official media. As a result, we stopped watching state television and opted instead to watch only foreign news broadcasts. However, I became increasingly concerned about the effects of this foreign television on our morals because Saudi Arabia has an Islamic tradition that must not be abandoned. Things got even worse; soon we had American troops setting up bases in Saudi Arabia. I find it difficult to understand – even now – how or why the American infidels with large numbers of immoral women were supposed to be protecting us. It was also difficult for me to reconcile the presence of these troops with the role of Saudi Arabia as the protector of Islam. After all, Allah has entrusted us with the holiest cities of Mecca and Medina. We felt betrayed; the Saudi government invested our oil money in large amounts of military equipment that we saw paraded frequently on the television screens, and now we discovered that it was ineffective. We have no real power to stand against Saddam Hussein. We had believed the authorities' claim that our military was so powerful it could stand against Israel but, subhan-Allah – *the wonders of the Almighty who will help us – we still need to understand how the Americans have come to be in charge.*

Another event that gripped my attention was a violent clash on the border near Jordan but in Saudi territory. It was an event relayed to us by my eldest brother Adel. I was shocked when he told me that some people were trying to smuggle alcohol across the border into Saudi Arabia. Luckily, the police were tipped off and launched a ghara *(raid). One of the smugglers was badly wounded but survived the attack. I remember how I listened to the details of this event with so much passion and alarm. To think that alcohol and corruption can slip into our land horrified me.*

After having completed my secondary schooling in Sakaka, I went to King Saud University in Riyadh, where I stayed with my paternal uncle, Badr. Riyadh, our capital, is huge and modern. At first I felt very proud of the development of the roads, the buildings, the hospitals and technology. I felt as if I had travelled to the most advanced country in the world. But I also felt a culture shock. I opted to study shari'a, *wanting to broaden my knowledge of the Islamic faith, as it is our gift from Allah and our ultimate shield. The following year, I returned to Sakaka and married my first paternal cousin, Jawhara, a very modest and pious young girl three years my junior. Jawhara had been assigned to me in marriage through an agreement between my father and my uncle, his brother. As a* salafi, *her looks were not at all an important consideration. I had not really seen her face before the wedding day. I was mostly attracted by her devotion to Islam and I was aware that I was completing half of my religious duty by getting married. I then returned with my wife to Riyadh to continue my university education. We stayed in a room made available to us by my uncle Badr. I felt so happy after my marriage; it gave me a feeling of security and of being protected against the sins and the possibility of the devil tempting me to commit* haram *(a religiously forbidden act). Jawhara was as shocked as I was by the physical size of Riyadh. If it were not for her* iman *(faith) she would have been devastated by the separation from her mother, sisters and other female relations.*

Three months into our marriage, Jawhara became pregnant. Although this meant that there were practical considerations to be taken care of – insofar as having a new family member was concerned – I was confident that Allah would provide for both my wife and the child. We know that each child brings his rizq *(provisions) with him. What I had to concentrate on during this time was learning about the* shari'a *at university. However, it was during this time that my frustrations and disillusionment with the Saudi system began to grow; a big wave of corruption, indecency and immorality was sweeping across the country, and it was up to me and other true believers to do something about it.*

In my second year at the university, I met and became very close friends with another university student called Sa'ad, from Qasim. We shared the same sentiments, most important of which was the desire for the uli al-amr *to change their ways regarding governance. Another concern of ours was the state of the* umma *(Islamic nation). I found it deeply disturbing that my other cousins cared little about this; they were running around Riyadh buying Western music and thinking that advancement and technology could only be adopted through Western ways of corruption. One day I saw my cousin Abdul Ilah clapping his hands during a football match. 'Are we Westerners?', I asked him. 'Are we effeminate?' I felt ashamed because we all know that clapping the hands in emotional excitement is behaviour only for women. As I got to know Sa'ad better, he introduced me to the writings of Sheikh Safar al-Hawali, his sermons and audio-tapes. We also met regularly with other young men with similar* concerns in a house belonging to one of Sa'ad's friends.

In that year I witnessed yet another event which proved to be a major turning point in my life. In September 1994, I found myself involved in a demonstration with many thousands of people. They were protesting against Saudi Arabia's rapid descent into the hands of non-believers and the contamination of the faith leading to the ultimate destruction of the social order which had underpinned Saudi society. The demonstration took place in the town of Buraida. Both the leaders of the demonstration, Sheikh Salman al-'Oda and Sheikh Safar al-Hawali, were arrested by the authorities. My friend Sa'ad and several others were among those also arrested. As far as I was concerned, this was further proof of the real intentions of the Saudi ruling establishment. There was no doubt in my mind that they were manipulating Islam for their own political advantage and not that of the umma; reform was the last thing they wanted to see. They were squandering the country's money by giving it to the American infidels, in effect depriving their own people. They have no concept of accountability towards the umma.

After the Buraida incident, I returned to my uncle's house in Riyadh feeling that I had fulfilled part of my duty towards my umma. I have taken risks by expressing my solidarity with the leaders of the Islamic reform movement. I could do this because I knew my home was secure. Jawhara made sure that all was taken care of; she kept her place as a woman, only engaging in activities that were related to female or household occupations, in addition to paying respects to elders and never interfering in that which does not concern her.

By the end of my second year at university, I had become very worried about what was in store for us as Saudi Arabians. Not only was I upset about the inconsistency of the welfare system but it was also becoming evident that only people living in Saudi Arabia's main cities had been privileged and been given resources by the state. Others had succumbed to the temptation of rashwa (bribery). The only way people can survive is by relying on their family, not on the government.

You could see evidence of social corruption and malaise on the streets, in Riyadh and elsewhere across Saudi Arabia. The wealthy had huge palaces built in expensive marble which were empty while other people were left in need. This is definitely an unfair distribution of Allah's wealth. You could also see corruption in the market-places, with women *hardly conforming to the dress code as prescribed by the* shariʿa, *their faces uncovered, showing Western make-up, and mixing freely with men. In the shops that sell music you saw foreign men, especially Filipinos, casually chatting with Saudi men and women buying music that not only was* mulhi *(a distraction from the faith) but also had nothing to do with our own values and traditions. Western women were allowed to roam around unveiled, setting a bad example for our own women. Even more worrying was the immorality that had become so pervasive in Saudi society; the mixing of the sexes, the laughter, the party-going. It was as if Western society had been imposed on Saudi society. Even the* mutawʿa *do not have the resources or power to clamp down on this kind of widespread immorality and religious corruption.*

Because of this degradation of Islamic morality, and the authorities' idle reaction to it, I took it upon myself to become a mutawiʿ. *At least in this way I could reprimand people for not conforming to* salafi *principles and traditions. At the same time, I continued to learn more about the* shariʿa. *In this way, I built upon my knowledge of Islam and did my utmost to help reverse the process of moral and religious degradation. We must fulfil our duty to do what is right.*

Jawhara gave birth to a baby girl in 1996, and to another baby girl the following year. Though I am grateful to Allah for blessing me with these two girls, I am looking forward to having my first son. As we Muslims know, 'You want and I want, but ultimately Allah will fulfil his will.'

Since completing my university education, I have continued in my role as a volunteer mutawiʿ. *So far, I have failed to find a suitable job in which I can make use of my university education. I refuse to compromise my principles by accepting the ridiculous jobs that are advertised in the newspapers. These are to fool people, for example 'Zahrani al-Zahrani' helping to manage a hotel in Jeddah. The Saudi system seems to have completely failed to serve those for whom it was originally set up. The best jobs are taken up by the Americans and the English because our government goes out of its way to cater to their governments' every need. I do not mind the presence of other Muslim expatriate workers, but I think it is unnecessary to have such large numbers of Filipino workers. It is clear that many changes must be made to save our country. But even more importantly, we need to rescue our society and traditions from further moral decay. Our 'sultan' must listen to our demands before it is too late.*

In order to provide for our children, I know that I have to learn English, the language of the infidels, to help understand the complexity of our world. Life's necessities dictate that I have to do this to learn to operate a computer in order to get a job. Since I cannot do this without proficiency in English I will master the skill, and one day, Allah willing, together with my friends I will save the umma.

Muna's story

My name is Muna. I am a Saudi Arabian woman. I was born in 1976 in the city of Buraida. I am the only daughter of my mother and father. My five brothers have always bullied me, but I guess that taught me to stand up for myself and not to rely on anyone else for protection.

My father's name is Suleiman. He had always been a government employee but, through wasta, *managed to change his job and become a personnel manager in Aramco oil company. Initially, he was working in the local municipality in Buraida. My mother is called Noora. She is a housewife. Actually I have never got on well with her; she has always preferred my brothers over me. The problem seems to have become compounded when she was unable to accept and relate to my developing mind and femininity.*

I first went to school in Buraida. As the only girl in the family, I was treated very strictly. My parents allowed my brothers to go out after school while I had to sit and wait for some of our relatives to visit us. This was the only form of entertainment at the time. It was virtually impossible for me to visit any of my classmates, as most were not related to me.

When I was thirteen, I caught a glimpse of my best friend's brother. Lou'loua told me that he was her favourite brother and that his name was Hamad. After that, he started following me home, undeterred by the risk of being seen by one of my brothers. We also managed to exchange telephone numbers and started calling each other regularly. Soon, my brother Abdallah discovered this and became enraged. As a result, life became like a living hell at home; because I caused shame to the family, my mother took an oath that I was to stay at home, and I was banned from going to school for the rest of the academic year.

The following year, God answered my prayers for an escape. Through the wasta of a distant cousin who had studied in the United States and held a senior position in the petrochemical industry, my father was offered a very respectable job at Aramco in Dhahran. We moved to a new world with so many Americans; it was amazing – the women even drove cars. I went to a local school. We were still in the process of settling into our new surroundings when the Iraqi invasion of Kuwait took place. Within a matter of days, Dhahran became centre-stage for the allies' war effort against Iraq.

Although I was sad that the war was taking place and that the Kuwaitis had their country usurped by another, I was nonetheless thrilled to see many aspects of the war effort taking place on our doorstep. For example, among the American troops there were many women soldiers. Kuwaiti women also arrived across the border driving cars. Only we, the Saudi women, remain backward and forbidden from doing many things that are taken for granted by women in other countries, even Islamic ones.

After things calmed down, I enjoyed school, till one day, when I was sixteen, my parents announced that I was to marry my cousin, Mansour, who was coming from Buraida. The thought of marrying someone whom I didn't even know, whom I found completely unattractive – not to mention the risk of having children with a very close blood relation, and, to top it all, returning to Buraida – was absolutely harrowing. After much fighting within the family, my father persuaded my mother that it would be improper according to shari'a *to force a woman to get married against her will.*

When I was only seventeen, one of the students gave me a book by Ihssan Abul Qaddus titled ana hurra *(I Am Free). The book opened my eyes to an entirely new world with limitless possibilities. My world was even further expanded after my family decided to follow many other families in Dhahran and purchase a satellite dish. I was glued to our television set, enjoying the offerings of foreign programmes. It was also at this time that I took up painting. My friend Farida, whose mother is Lebanese, gave me a set of paints. I started painting women as I saw them on the television and walking on the street without veils, with their hair flying in the wind; but behind them I drew chains.*

At the end of the school year, my school had arranged an exhibition of the students' art work. Most other paintings were of the desert, the sun, the sea, mountain ranges or just fruits, most especially the apple! These things I found inexplicably boring. I still cannot understand why the apple was so popular. Anyway, my mother was quite appalled when she set her eyes upon my latest pictures. She started apologizing to everyone about my paintings, which I was very proud of.

I graduated from secondary school when I was eighteen years old. It was during that summer that a very unfortunate event took place. I was with Farida in a supermarket in Dhahran, where Filipinos served. Farida introduced me to two American women, one of whom worked as a nurse at Aramco. Though both were wearing the 'abaya (the woman's black cloak) they both had their hair uncovered. Farida followed suit, and I did as well, taking advantage of what appeared to be all-foreign surroundings. While we were laughing – and I must admit I got carried away with the chatter – to my horror, a mutawi' *followed by two policemen suddenly appeared and questioned me about my identity. I started trembling with fear and could not answer their questions. They said: 'hurma! Woman! Are you a Muslim? Woman! Don't you have men to protect you?' Within minutes, I had been shoved into one of the* al-hay'a's *cars, together with Farida, who was doing her best with her Lebanese accent to gain their sympathy. We were locked up at the* al-hay'a *headquarters until the early hours of the morning when my father arrived, accompanied by my brother Abdullah, who was visibly in pain and suffering from feelings of shame. The* mutaw'a *proceeded to talk about the importance of maintaining and preserving the sanctity of Islam and of Islamic traditions: they made it clear that they would not tolerate any act that would desecrate the holy traditions of our religion and country. They referred to an American plot and other Western corrupting influences, from which Saudi women had to be protected. My father then reassured them about the importance of Islamic values and told them that he would put me on the right path and added that I was still very young, ignorant and naïve. I was so afraid that I cannot remember much of what happened later, especially after my return home. My mother was hysterical, from both worry and shame. My brother Abdullah argued with my father that had I married my cousin Mansour, the family would have been spared the shame of my behaviour.*

I spent the next few months watching satellite television and continued painting, knowing that my friends had started attending university. I was depressed and not eating very much, becoming weaker by the day. The doctor said that I needed a change of environment. It was at this point that my maternal aunt, who is very open-minded compared with my mother, invited me to spend a couple of months in London. My aunt speaks fluent English because she lives in London with her husband, who works at the embassy.

After having spent some time in London, I came across someone I knew, whom qadar *(fate) had brought my way. One day, while I was at Whiteley's, that exciting department store with cinemas and restaurants, we exchanged looks, words and then telephone numbers. Salem started talking to me regularly and we liked each other's ideas. Salem is from Qahtan in the Asir region, known in Saudi Arabia to be very tribally oriented and far away from the heart of Nejd. He is studying for a Master's degree at London University. I would escape from my aunt's house without her knowing that it was to meet Salem. As she was constantly busy with female functions at the embassy, I had lots of time to spend with Salem. However, I soon found out that he never contemplated marrying me. To him, I was a loose* bint, *to be seen and talked to without entering into any formal relationship. My struggle with tradition bothered him, and despite his intelligence and Western education, he wants the mother of his children to be absolutely traditional. I felt devastated.*

My family want me to conform by marrying my first cousin; the modern man I met and want to marry is himself obsessed with notions of tradition and is only superficially modern. My mother was lucky to have married a good man and moved to a modern city like Dhahran, but she's too uptight about what is wrong and what is right for her to enjoy anything. I certainly do not see myself fulfilling my mother's role, giving birth to six children and not aspiring to study and work.

At my aunt's house I met an Egyptian woman who works for the Middle East Broadcasting Company. We immediately became friends and she encouraged me to work in the media. I am aware that for a girl from Buraida, from a tribal background, to expose her hair uncovered on television would be considered sacrilegious. At the moment, I am going through a very tense time. While I aspire to continue my studies, learn more English, work in the media and build a career for myself, my family is desperate for me to be married since they consider me to be almost an old maid. Thank God they don't know about Salem, even though our relationship is a hopeless one. He will probably end up marrying his first cousin from Qahtan.

The time has come for me to go back to Saudi Arabia. I wish I could run away and escape but after all, it is my country; there is nothing I can do about it. My father promised me that I can go to university. I plan to study English literature, hoping that I will be able to pursue, at some point in the future, a career in the media.

Revisiting Muhammad's story

Muhammad represents the pragmatist group, which forms the majority of Saudi youth. In this respect, he is an average member of the new middle classes. He is of non-tribal family origin and hence free from the tribal links that connect large areas of the rural hinterland into the main urban centres of the country. But although tribalism is not an issue for him, regionalism is. Muhammad is a Hijazi. When he moved to Riyadh from Jeddah he found the Nejdi environment dry and rigid. But his regional distinctiveness became diffused when he began training with a British engineering firm. This meant that Muhammad felt the influence of 'global culture' was more overwhelming than the regional differences he first experienced between Hijazis and Nejdis. Nevertheless, he still identifies himself and is indeed identified by his fellow Saudis as a Hijazi. He takes pride in his ability to adapt and cope with change. This he explains by reference to the fact that Hijazis have always belonged to a hetero-geneous culture based around a comparatively multicultural society that continued to be exposed to the annual waves of pilgrims flooding into the holy places. His family are from Bahra, which is on the route between Jeddah and Mecca. This, he believes, has given him more exposure than the average Saudi. He was brought up in Jeddah, the main port of Saudi Arabia, which has always been cosmopolitan and heterogeneous, receiv-ing pilgrims and commerce from India, Egypt and Africa. Despite his proud reference to being a Hijazi, there is no doubt that Muhammad perceives himself to be first and foremost a Saudi. National identity has become a dominant component of his sense of belonging. For him, as for other members of the new generation, national identity is not a conscious interest-driven decision but an integral part of his consciousness.

The new generation – an overview

The three composite members of the new generation have all travelled widely within Saudi Arabia. Muna moved from Buraidah to Dhahran, Abdul Rahman from Sakaka to Riyadh and Muhammad from Jeddah to Riyadh. This does not imply that most Saudis move to the capital. But the political economy of Saudi Arabia means that the centre of political, economic and religious power is located in Riyadh, the established core of the country, and radiates outwards from there. The movement of these young people away from their home towns reflects the social and geographic mobility that has been driven by oil wealth and the growth and consolidation of a national economy.

Although the dominant oil industry is in the eastern province and the holiest cities, Mecca and Medina, are in the Hijaz, the Al-Saud family have been successful in centring power and, to a great extent, legitimacy in Nejd. The new generation still remains part of large families. As typical young people, Abdul Rahman, Muna and Muhammad would have a family averaging seven members. Their parents' generation reaped the benefits of modern medicine with a drastic reduction of infant mortality in comparison with their own parents' generation. However, those among the new generation who are old enough to have children show signs of producing smaller families. The increased stress of following a career combined with economic pressures means that more and more women are delaying motherhood and limiting the number of children they have. Likewise, traditional kinship and marriage patterns are changing. The increased geographic mobility of young Saudi workers, though limited in comparison with other Middle Easterners, is loosening ties to the extended family.

Everyone interviewed recognized that living standards are lower than those of the previous two generations. In relation to this, the fatalists still have hope that conditions might improve, the realists are voicing expressions of dissatisfaction and calling for economic reforms, while the activists, who remain a minority, believe that corruption and mismanagement should be treated in an Islamic manner. Since there are no organized channels of political expression, no arenas within which groups can convene and no clubs except for the *shilla* (a peer grouping based on gender), the mosques are the only outlet. This tends to mean that the emerging organized religious dissent takes on the form of radical neo-*wahhabi* movements. A large majority of those not pragmatically or radically involved in trying to better their circumstances are grumpy, bored and dissatisfied. But they have not been politicized partly because of their educational background and the system of patriarchy and hierarchy that successfully lays down strict rules about permissible behaviour.

The new generation is also aware of the privileges acquired as a spin-off from the oil boom. The children of the new middle class, who are a direct product of great social mobility, see the difference in their living standards and mores from those of their parents. While they recognize that their parents lived in a period of oil wealth, they themselves have more information and know-how. A central problem that keeps emerging in discussions is that of *wasta,* influence and government contacts. The majority of those interviewed are critical of this practice, and yet they realize that they need it to survive. What many increasingly object to is the fact that despite their qualifications or professional abilities, they can only get jobs through *wasta.* The meritocratic approach their education has led them to expect sits uncomfortably with the use of *wasta* that still permeates the governing system and society at large.

A major issue of rising social and economic tension is the continuous presence of the expatriates, who constitute the majority of the workforce. Attitudes towards the expatriate community are characterized by increasing antagonism and racism. The fatalists consider their presence to be inevitable, albeit annoying. The realists take a more aggressive stance towards foreign workers but are critical of the failures of the Saudi-ization programme. To them, foreigners are categorized according to profession and the perceived needs of Saudi society. As for the Islamists, they believe that all foreigners, as long as they are Muslim, are acceptable as part of the workforce. Their reservations are directed at the non-Muslims. The crucial question for the new generation remains, are Saudi youth willing and technically able to do both the menial and the skilled tasks that are currently undertaken by the expatriate workforce? The realistic answer to this question in the short to medium term will be troubling for the self-esteem of the new generation. At bottom, the new generation as a whole is not politicized, and the majority are in no way politically active. However, there is a detectable change in attitudes towards the government. The government has become the 'other' that many no longer trust. As the population grew and the government became more institutionalized, access to the influential rulers declined. Although some members of the new generation still have access to younger, university-educated but less influential princes, there is an increasing questioning of patronage, accompanied by demands for liberty, equality and transparency. The role of the king's *majlis* has traditionally provided the image of benevolent patrons, promoting a process of consultation. As state patrimony comes under increased economic strain, this image no longer bears much resemblance to the everyday experiences of the new generation. Thus methods of coercion through the deployment and threatened removal of largesse are weakening. Patron–client relations are shaken as a result. This in turn places a strain on the foundations of national government. The whole system based upon the capacity of the elite at the head of the government to reward and punish cannot function in the same way. These changes have led to the young describing the government in terms starkly different from those expressed by their parents. Although they still believe in the achievements of the Saudi state, they realize the limitations of what the government can do for them. To the conservatives, relations with the West, and with the United States, in particular exacerbate feelings of vulnerability and mistrust.

This study has attempted to document and analyse what the youth have said about Saudi society, its government and their own hopes for the future. There is a prevailing nostalgia, with the dominant belief that government was much better under previous rulers. The remarks of many interviewees revolve around a feeling of being peripheral both to the state and to society at large; a widespread criticism is of being ignored. They want some form of participation in the governing process and wish to feel that their genuine concerns are at least being listened to by the authorities.

The constant theme that runs through all the interviews is the new generation's desire for freedom from constraints, whether overtly political or more generally social. Irrespective of whether they are conservative, liberal, Islamists, rich or poor, male or female, all those interviewed express a general desire for greater freedom, for more space in which to articulate their wants and needs. The issue of double standards is of great concern to the youth. Their expectations are marked by a great sense of loss when they reflect on the benefits their parents regarded as their right but which are now seen as increasingly hard to obtain. Ultimately, their expectations of what the state should and should not do appear to be influenced by ideas from outside Saudi society. These ideas concern progress, trade and education. Generally, members of the new generation, replete with a definite sense of national identity, want their country to thrive, but in tandem with this they want the space within Saudi society to develop their own attitudes and opinions without the overbearing presence of the state and *'ulama*.

Appendix: fieldwork methodology

Introduction

In Saudi Arabia and the wider Gulf, politics are too often studied only at the state level and above. Although the social and political constraints on research make this understandable, such an approach often results in general and detached findings that give limited insight into the functioning of Gulf societies. To redress the balance, considerations of political stability in Saudi Arabia need to take serious account of domestic factors by using the tools of social anthropology as opposed to those of policy studies and international relations. The connection between culture and politics in the Saudi context cannot be underestimated, especially given the increasing politicization of the country's new generation. The research project which gave rise to this book deliberately set out to give a voice to the most important but frequently overlooked section of Saudi Arabia, the youth. It is hoped that this approach will assist in building a more nuanced understanding of Saudi Arabia with a greater awareness of the everyday concerns and opinions of its young population.

This book is structured around a central theme, the creation and continual transformation of identity. The broad theoretical assumptions of this approach are explored in Chapter 1. Each of the subsequent chapters attempts to explore and develop this theme by looking at subjects such as education and their influence on the identity of the new generation in Saudi Arabia. The theme of identity arose through an interaction among the fieldwork observations, interviews and wider concerns expressed in three types of academic literature – social anthropology, political science and historical works specific to the Gulf region. In planning and carrying out this research programme I was greatly helped by the experience and knowledge I had obtained on previous fieldwork for my PhD in Saudi Arabia between 1985 and 1987. This project has allowed me to renew old friendships and pursue new lines of enquiry. The resulting book is primarily a study of the opinions, attitudes, motivations and aspirations of the new generation. The empirical research offers an account of how the spectrum of Saudi youth interviewed perceives the cultural, political and economic forces that are transforming their lives and the societies of the Gulf region.

The approach to researching in Saudi Arabia

Since September 1997, I have been continually interviewing Saudi Arabian youth between the ages of fifteen and thirty in an attempt to gauge the effects of increased economic insecurity and exposure to the globalization of culture. As a research methodology, I used participant observation, focusing on both group and individual interviews. The interviews lasted between one and three hours without interruption. Some interviews were supplemented by telephone conversations or by repeat visits.

The questions asked were divided into broad categories dependent on age, with individuals being asked the same question irrespective of their background or gender. The questions in each category encompassed various themes, including education, vocational aspirations, exposure to different cultural influences, access to information, derivation of values, generational differences, approaches to problem-solving and future prospects. When conducting the interviews, I used open-ended questions, allowing the young people to raise and develop issues that had not been previously defined. This lack of rigidity was intended to allow the interviewees to talk about matters which they perceived as important.

The interviews were carried out largely in Saudi Arabia, although a minority were also conducted in Washington, Boston and London, reflecting the seasonal movements of upper-class Saudis and the location of favoured educational establishments, as well as educational centres where some middle-class youth were training. By conducting limited interviews outside the Kingdom, I also gained an insight into the extent to which personal freedom of expression increased when Saudis travelled abroad.

Most interviews were conducted entirely in Arabic, although those interviewees who were fluent in English tended to answer in a mixture of English and Arabic, as is their habit in conversation. I used a notebook to write down their main answers, and this was backed up whenever agreeable by a tape recorder. I tended to use a tape recorder more in the limited number of group interviews I conducted, especially those at schools. The degree of openness was related to who was present when the interview was conducted; for example, if older members of the family, or teachers, were present, the interviewees became more constrained than when interviewed separately or with their peer group. The background and education of the interviewees also affected the openness and trust shown to the ethnographer.

My identity as a Saudi female academic, older than the young people interviewed, was a source of cooperation and trust. My gender allowed me access to both men and women, whereas a man could generally only interview other men. Social concepts of honour and shame mean that most women would not agree to meet and converse with men who were not family members. While the reverse is also possible, normally Saudi men will agree to be interviewed by a female researcher, especially when maintaining the appropriate formalities such as dress code and language. Only two men refused to talk to me in person; lengthy interviews were conducted over the telephone. Both men considered themselves to be radical *salafis* who observe strict gender segregation. However, the majority of the middle class and merchants were eager to be interviewed.

Inevitably, the presence of the ethnographer caused behaviour to be modified to a degree. There were times when I was aware of the interviewees telling me what they thought I would like to hear; for example, 'I would not object to my wife working, but ...'; or defending me in a group interview when one of the youth criticized me for not wearing the *hijab*.

Overall, I deployed a standard approach to research, aiming to engage my interviewees in debate and discussion. I found the youth, both men and women, eager to talk and express their problems, frustrations, hopes and desires. Those members of the new generation to whom I had the privilege of talking were friendly, supportive and very encouraging. In this context, some expressed a desire to be consulted on a wider basis, to be asked for their opinions by the authorities and decision-makers in the same way that I asked them questions about who they are and how they think they can solve problems. They took pride in talking about their country and boasted to others that they were being interviewed and consulted for a book as 'important citizens' and even as the 'future decision-makers' of Saudi Arabia. The book is constructed mainly around the words of those interviewed, and I have clearly indicated where their interpretations and my own differ.

The research has attempted to explore the new generation's own interpretations of the constraints and choices it faces. The length of time interviewing each subject and the type of questioning used meant that it was not possible to conduct large-scale surveys. The approach adopted deliberately sought to prioritize quality over quantity, allowing a deeper insight into the tensions and ambiguities of young people's position in Saudi Arabia.

Given the wide range of people interviewed it was inevitable that I would encounter different and competing views and perceptions of the world. The initial findings from the interviews were often contradictory, with little coherence. Only when the outline of the picture emerged could I identify the missing pieces. I was confronted with very idealistic accounts of life and views of the future which appeared to contradict the situations in which these young people found themselves. But overall these sometimes stark contradictions between ideal and reality were themselves indicative of the social tensions induced by rapid and disorientating change which the last three generations of the Saudi population have experienced.

The background to the interviewees

During the research process I tried to interview as broad a sample of Saudi society as possible. Those interviewed can be loosely categorized in seven overlapping groups that make up Saudi society:

(1) Young people who belong to the royal family, both those close to the throne and those on the periphery.
(2) Those whose families are powerful politically and whose relatives are high-ranking state functionaries.
(3) Those related to key trading and business families.

(4) Those who can loosely be described as belonging to the intelligentsia or 'educated class', including people who have spent an extended time in higher education and others whose parents are or who are themselves working in education-related employment, as well as journalists, poets and authors.

(5) Those who belong to the new middle class – the largest single sector of the population, including managers, administrators, technicians, teachers and low-and middle-ranking army officers. Their welfare and work depend directly and solely on state employment and they rarely travel abroad in comparison to the Saudi elite. The new middle class are differentiated into an upper and a lower stratum. The upper stratum comprises the more educated members of the Saudi population, for example, doctors and high-ranking engineers, whereas the lower stratum is represented by government clerical personnel, school teachers and skilled industrial wage-earners.

(6) Those of rural origin or who have recently emigrated from the countryside into the cities, including some of the poorest sections of Saudi society, whose levels of literacy and standards of living are well below the national average.

(7) Religious activists and graduates from the Islamic university sectors, who, by social origins, obviously derive from one or other of the first six categories.

In an attempt to summarize the range of backgrounds of those within each group I have listed a representative sample of those I have encountered over the last two years of interviewing. Furthermore, all those listed have had their names altered to protect their identities. The ages of the interviewees are those at the time of interview. The overall aim is to make the origins and opinions of those whom I interviewed clearer without endangering the promise of anonymity that made the research possible.

The royal family

Ghada (15) is a member of the Saudi royal family. She has been studying in Europe for three years. **Noura** (16), her sister, is also studying abroad.

Noura wants to get married after graduating from university and have five children.

Mansour (30) is a direct descendant of the founder of the Kingdom, Abdul Aziz Al-Saud. Mansour has lived most of his life in Saudi Arabia, where after graduating he went on to specialize in a military academy. He then attended a European military academy before enrolling in a prestigious British university for a Master's degree in social science.

Nouf (23), from Riyadh, is a member of a section of the royal family close to the throne. Both her father and mother are of Al-Saud decent. Nouf has many brothers and sisters, but only has four *ashiqaa'* (full brothers). The five siblings appear to enjoy close relations, and Nouf says that she was spoiled as the only girl. She went to a private school and on to a state university in Saudi Arabia.

Non-royal families with political influence

Abdul Rahman (18), from Riyadh, is representative of families with political influence. His father is in a position of power close to the royal family. His mother is university-educated and of non-Saudi Muslim origin. The father has a BA from the United States. Abdul Rahman is the eldest of four children, two girls and two boys. He started his education in a private school in Saudi Arabia before going on to university in the United States.

Jawahir (15) is the eldest of five children. She is from a prestigious tribal Nejdi background and is connected by marriage to the royal family. Her father works for the government and her mother is a housewife.

Salman (25) is from Ahsa. His father has had a long career in the upper echelons of government, close to the royal family, and hence at the centre of decision-making power. His mother is European and has always been a housewife. Salman studied at private school, then left Saudi Arabia for university in Europe.

Prominent merchant families

Abdul Muhsin (26), from Najran, is the son of a prominent businessman from a key merchant family. His mother died when he was very young and his father married his deceased wife's sister, a customary practice; hence Abdullah was brought up by his maternal aunt. He studied at a private school and then went to university in the United States, where he also undertook postgraduate studies.

Dania (24), from Jeddah, is the younger of two children. Her father is a businessman from a prominent merchant family. Her mother is also from an established business family; she was educated in Egypt but has never worked. Dania went to *dar al-hanan* (House of Tenderness) private school and then to university.

Faiz (16), from Ahsa, is the first-born of two children. His father is an educated, successful, wealthy businessman. His mother is also from a business family and has a university degree, although she has chosen to remain a housewife. Faiz studied at *dar al-fikr* school in Jeddah until the last year of his secondary education, which he spent in the United States.

Faris (16) has one brother. His father is from Qasim and is a senior manager in a large Saudi company. Faris's mother is from Medina and is a housewife. Faris is a student at a private school in Dhahran.

Layla (15), from the eastern province, has two brothers. Her father is a businessman and her mother a housewife. Layla is a student at a private school and has travelled widely with her parents.

Naif (23), from Medina, has a brother and sister. His father is a businessman and his mother is of non-Saudi Arab descent. His secondary education was in *madaris al-riyadh* and he gained undergraduate and postgraduate degrees from universities in the United States.

Rasha (27), from Mecca, says that she is 'distinctive' for having a non-Saudi Arab mother. She is one of six full siblings, and has a further five siblings on her father's side. She considers herself a Hijazi. Her educational background has been cosmopolitan, with schooling in Lebanon, Switzerland and the United Kingdom

Suhair (27) comes from the south of Saudi Arabia. Her father is a prominent businessman, well connected to the ruling elite. Suhair's family comes from a minority religious sect. Her mother died when she was in her early teens, after which her father married her mother's sister. Suhair is one of many children from her father's numerous marriages, mostly to relatives. She studied at *dar al-hanan* school and then at King Abdul Aziz university.

Sundus (23), from Mecca, is one of four children. Her father is a businessman and both parents are from prominent business families in Jeddah. Sundus studied at *dar al-hanan* school in Jeddah and at a university in the United States.

The intelligentsia

Ahmed (21), from Jeddah, has two younger sisters. Both his parents were educated at universities in the United Kingdom. His mother is a non-Arab Muslim. His patrilineal family are not wealthy, but come from an old Arab lineage. Ahmed completed his secondary school education at *al-thaghr* private school in Jeddah, after which he attended a British military academy, following in the footsteps of his father. Ahmed is currently studying law in Britain.

Amani (15) comes from the eastern province, Ahsa. Her father is an academic/businessman who runs a private school in Saudi Arabia. She has studied for two years in the United Kingdom.

Amina (18) is a first-generation Saudi from Hadramout. She was born in Jeddah and is the second of three children. Amina's father holds several degrees from British universities. Her mother is a non-Saudi Muslim and is also a university graduate. Amina completed secondary school at *madaris al-fardous*, after which she was sent to a British university.

157

Asma (28) studied at *dar al-hanan* private school in Jeddah and then attended King Abdul Aziz University. After her graduation she worked at the same university in an administrative capacity.

Ghalib (17) is of tribal descent and one of five children. His mother is a Hijazi Sharifa (from the previous Ashraf ruling elite) from Mecca. His father is studying abroad for a PhD, so his mother divides her time between her husband and her family in Saudi Arabia. Ghalib is a first-year student at university in Saudi Arabia.

Jamila, Asia, Amel and **Ahlam** are first cousins aged between 18 and 21. Jamila and Asia are the daughters of a university lecturer who has a PhD in science from a British university; their mother works in higher education administration. All four girls studied at d*ar al-hanan* private school and then at King Abdul Aziz University.

Malak (17) is a first-generation Saudi, born in Jeddah, and the youngest of three children. Malak's father is from the royal family of Hadramout, who settled in Saudi Arabia for political reasons; he has degrees from British universities. Her mother is a non-Saudi Muslim and also graduated from British universities. Malak attended *al-ferdous* private school in Jeddah and has just started university in Cairo.

Maryam (27) is the second of three sisters (the third is from a different father). Her father is a first-generation Saudi from Malaysia who settled with a Meccan family and was educated at a university in Egypt. Her father is a civil servant; her mother had no formal education but has travelled widely. Maryam was educated at *dar al-hanan* school in Jeddah and has gone on to do postgraduate work at a university in the United States.

Mish'al (29), from Riyadh, is the first-born of five children. His father is a medical doctor and although his mother has a university degree, she has always been a housewife. His family are self-consciously modern and liberal in their lifestyle, which they advertise by, for instance, eating out at restaurants in Jeddah such as *al-nakhil* (The Palm Trees). Mish'al was educated at the Capital Institute in Riyadh and then at an American university.

Saad (16) is of Hijazi tribal descent. He is one of six children. His father has a PhD and is currently a senior educational administrator. His mother has never worked but he describes her as 'a very strong woman'. Saad wants to study archaeology at university and then lecture and write books.

The new middle class

Abdul Ilah (23), from Riyadh, is the first-born of seven children. His father is a retired military official. Abdul Ilah went to state school in Riyadh and then started training at a vocational institute after a year of unemployment.

Abdul Hamid (23), from Hail, is one of seven children. He studied at a state school in Riyadh and is currently training for one year with a British firm. His father is a civil servant.

Abdul Karim (23), from Al Qasim, is one of ten children from more than one mother. His father is a retired military official. Abdul Karim studied at a state school in Riyadh after he dropped out of state university to train as an engineer.

Abdul Wahid (24), from Albaha, is the eldest of eight children. His father works for the Ministry of Information. He is training as a mechanical engineer with a foreign company in Riyadh.

Abir (15) comes from the eastern province. Her father works for an oil company and her mother is a housewife. She is the eldest of five children and is a student. Abir wants to marry a Saudi after her university education.

Adel (16) is from a southern Hijazi tribal background but has lived most of his life in Riyadh. His father is a civil servant. Adel is currently studying at *al-khosami,* a private school in Riyadh.

Adnan (24) comes from Mecca, where his family still live. Many among his extended family have left Mecca, especially the more successful. Adnan is the first-born of five children and wishes that his mother would have more children. His father is a government employee and his mother a housewife. Their marriage was arranged. Adnan studied at *al-thanawiyya* state school in Mecca and then at King Abdul Aziz University in Jeddah.

Arif (27), from Riyadh, is one of nine children from two mothers. His deceased father was a businessman. Arif studied at a state school in Riyadh and opted for vocational training as a mechanical engineer rather than going to university.

Ashwaq (15) is from Mecca. Her father works for the diplomatic service and her mother is a housewife. She has five sisters and brothers. Ashwaq is currently at school in London.

Ayman (16), from Riyadh, has one sister and one brother. His father is a civil servant and his mother a housewife. Ayman is a student at *al-khosami* private school and has travelled to the West with his family.

Daghas (23) is from Riyadh, where his father is a trader and owns a shop. Daghas is one of seven siblings. He studied at a state school in Riyadh, spent two years at university and then dropped out. He is now being trained as an aircraft maintenance engineer.

Dana (15) comes from Medina and is one of five children. Her father works for the diplomatic corps and her mother is a housewife. Dana studied at *al-tarbiyya al-haditha* private school in Jeddah and is currently at school in London.

Dunya (15), from Jeddah, has two sisters. Her father is a pilot with Saudia Airlines. Dunya speaks foreign languages because of her European mother and summers spent abroad.

Fahad (23), from Hail, in the north, is one of 14 children from three different mothers. Fahad did not get the grades required to enter university in Riyadh, so he is now in employment.

Fahda (15), from Riyadh, is attending a Saudi school in London, where her family are spending a couple of years. Her father is a civil servant.

She is one of five children. She wants to return to Riyadh and study at King Saud University.

Fawzi (15) comes from Taif and has six brothers and two sisters. His father is a government employee and his mother a housewife.

Ghazi (15) comes from the eastern province but has lived in Riyadh. His father is a government employee and his mother is a housewife. Ghazi is one of six children and a student at a state school.

Hadi (23), from Riyadh, is one of nine children. His father is a civil servant and his mother is a housewife. Hadi studied at a state school in Riyadh. He did not achieve the required average to study medicine at university, therefore he opted for training in computer science.

Haifa (16), from Riyadh, is the eldest of seven children. She is a *muhajjaba* and kept her head covered throughout the interview, even though there were no men present at the school.

Hani (18) is from Jeddah. He is one of five children. His father is a government employee and his mother a housewife. He wants to study computer science at a local university.

Hawazin (15), from Jeddah, is the fourth of five children. Her father is a second-generation Saudi of Arab–Southeast Asian descent whose family settled in Mecca and worked as *mutawwifin* (guides for the pilgrims). Her father studied abroad before becoming a government employee. Hawazin is a student at *al-furdous* private school.

Hiba (15) is from Medina. Her father is a civil servant and her mother is a housewife. Hiba wants to read computer studies at university but does not want to work. This is because 'studying is open to women but work is limited in Saudi Arabia'. Hiba wants to marry young and have six children.

Hind (19) was born in Jeddah although both her parents are first-generation Saudis from non-Arab Muslim backgrounds who settled in

Mecca. She is one of five children. Her father is a civil servant and her mother a housewife. Hind studied at *al-ferdous* private school in Jeddah and is currently studying medicine at King Abdul Aziz University.

Issam (21), from Yanbu, is the fifth of eleven children. His father is a retired engineer. Hisham did not get the required grades to enter university and so opted for a more specialized career training as an engineer.

Jassem (23) comes from Riyadh. He is one of seven children. His father is a civil servant. Jassem dropped out of university after two years, and after a year of unemployment he opted for vocational training in aeronautics.

Maha (17) is the first-born of seven children, five girls and two boys. Her father is an engineer and her mother is a housewife. Maha is a *muhajjaba*, even in an all-female environment.

Majid (23) comes from Taif. He is of central Asian descent and is physically distinctive, as the family intermarried with central Asian families. His father is a shopkeeper and his mother is a housewife. He is the second of eleven children, all from the same mother. Majid finished secondary school in Taif and then worked in a construction company in Yanbu. His ambition is to contribute to the development of his nation.

Manal (17) is one of five children, three boys and two girls. The family come from Hail but Manal lived in Jordan for many years because her father was based there.

Mun'im (24), from Riyadh, is one of six children. His father is a retired school teacher. Mun'in is training at a vocational institute.

Nader (16), from Mecca, is of southern Hijazi, tribal descent. He is one of five children. His father works as a civil servant and his mother is a housewife.

Noura (15) is one of five children. Her father is from Jeddah and works for Saudia Airlines. Her mother is European.

Omar (16) is from Jeddah. His father is a first-generation Saudi who currently works at a bank in Jeddah. His non-Arab mother is a school teacher. Omar is one of four children and goes to a state school in Jeddah.

Osama (16) is from Riyadh and one of six children. His father is a government employee and his mother is a housewife. Osama is studying at a state school.

Sahar (30) is from Jeddah. She is the eldest of three children, two girls and one boy. Her father worked in flight administration for Saudia Airlines for thirty-five years. Her mother is not educated and has always been a housewife. Sahar finished secondary education at *thanawiyya al-ula* state school. She did not go to university because she got married. Sahar is divorced and her father is encouraging her to find suitable employment.

Sami (30) is the first-born of two children. His father is a medical doctor and a first-generation Saudi from Southeast Asia with 'Arab blood'. Her mother is from Hijaz and has had a basic education. Sami defines herself as 'liberal' and has travelled abroad. Sami studied at a private school before going to university in the United States.

Samir (15), from Hail in the north of Saudi Arabia, is one of five children. His father works for the Saudi government. His mother graduated from a Saudi university, where she studied agriculture; she has never worked.

Sara (15), from Medina, is the eldest of four children. Her father works for Saudia Airlines and her mother is a housewife. She attends a private school.

Sultan (15), from Riyadh, is one of seven children. He has lived in London for two years with his paternal uncle, who works at the Saudi embassy. Although he has lived in London and attended school there (albeit a Muslim one), Sultan is unable to converse in English.

Thamer (15), from Riyadh, has one brother and one sister. His father is a senior civil servant and his mother a housewife. Thamer is a student at *riyadh al-khasa* private school.

Yassir (22) is from Riyadh and one of seven children. His father is an entrepreneur who travels a great deal. Yassir attended university for two years in Riyadh but did not complete his degree, choosing to specialize in mechanical engineering instead.

Youssef (15) is from Ras Tannoura. His father works in the petrochemical industry and his mother is a housewife. He has two sisters and a brother. Youssef want to go to university in Dhahran.

Those of rural background recently moved to the city

Said (27) is of recent rural Bedouin origin. He was born in Tabuk, where he lived until the age of eighteen, and is one of ten children. His grandfather was a *shaykh al-ashirah* and both his father and mother are illiterate.

Radical salafis or Islamic activists

Abdul Aziz (30), from Jeddah, has two brothers and three sisters. He studied for three years at King Abdul Aziz University, never graduated and was unemployed for a few years. He is married and has four children. His father is now retired but used to work for Saudia Airlines. After going into exile for fear of persecution because of his activist stance, Abdul Aziz undertook training in the field of computer science.

Hamad (29) comes from the southern tribes. His father was a businessman. He has four brothers and two sisters. Hamad has lived most of his life in Dammam, in the eastern province. He graduated from technical secondary school and worked for SABIC for six years.

The categories listed above do not encompass tribal affiliation or subnational geographic identities. These are noted only where relevant to the interviewees' ideas and sentiments. These sources of identity clearly tend to stretch across different groups. It is apparent, for example, that those from the Hijaz region are more heterogeneous in composition that other regions, sometimes with 'mixed blood'. I tried to achieve a balance in the interviews between the number of males and females in each category and overall, without, however, allowing gender definition to dominate the approach to research.

Bibliography

The Holy Quran, trans. Yousef Ali (Leicester: Islamic Foundation, 1975).

Abir, Mordechai, 'The Consolidation of the Ruling Class and the New Elites in Saudi Arabia', *Middle Eastern Studies*, Vol. 23, No. 2, 1987.

Abir, Mordechai, *Saudi Arabia in the Oil Era: Regime and Elites, Conflict and Collaboration* (London: Croom Helm, 1988).

Alani, Mustafa and Andrew Rathmell, 'Special Report', *Jane's Intelligence Review*, No. 2, 1996.

Altorki, Soraya, 'Women, Development and Employment in Saudi Arabia: The Case of 'Unayzah', *Journal of Developing Societies*, Vol. VIII, 1992, pp. 96–110.

Anderson, Benedict, *Imagined Communities: Reflections on the Origins and Spread of Nationalism* (London/New York: Verso, 1991, revised and extended edition).

'The Arab World and the Challenge of Globalisation', *The NCB Economist*, Vol. 27, No. 2, March/April 1997.

Arebi, Saddika, *Women and Words in Saudi Arabia* (New York: Columbia University Press, 1994).

Ayish, Mohammad I. and Ali Qassim, 'Direct Satellite Broadcasting in the Arab Gulf Region: Trends and Policies', *Gazette: International Journal for Mass Communication Studies*, Vol. 56, No. 1, 1995.

Al-Bassam, Ibtissam, A., 'Institutions of Higher Education for Women in Saudi Arabia', *International Journal of Educational Development*, Vol. 4, No. 3, 1984.

Birks, J. S., Seccombe, J. and C. A. Sinclair, 'Labour Migration in the Arab Gulf States: Patterns, Trends, and Prospects', *International Migration*, Vol. 26, No. 3, 1988, pp. 267–86.

Butter, David, 'Economic Recovery Puts Down Roots', *Middle East Economic Digest*, 3 January 1997.

Caufield, Catherine, *Masters of Illusion: The World Bank and the Poverty of Nations* (Basingstoke: Macmillan, 1997).

'Challenge to the House of Saud', *The Economist*, 8 October 1994.

Cohen, A. P., *Symbolic Construction of Community* (London: Routledge, 1985).

Cooper, John, 'The New Face of the Saudi State', *Middle East Economic Digest*, Vol. 39, No. 33, 18 August 1995.

Corzine, Robert and Michael Skapinker, 'Saudis Struggle to Pay for $7.5bn Airliner, Claim Bankers', *The Financial Times*, 3 November 1997.

Cunningham, Andrew, 'Post-war Blues', *The Banker*, September 1994.

Dean, Kathryn, *Politics and the Ends of Identity* (Aldershot, Hants: Ashgate, 1997).

Dekmejian, R. Hrair, *Islam in Revolution: Fundamentalism in the Arab World* (New York: Syracuse University Press, 1985).

Dekmejian, R. Hrair, 'The Rise of Political Islamism in Saudi Arabia', *Middle East Journal*, Vol. 48, No. 4, Autumn 1994.

Doumato, Eleanor Abdella, 'Women and the Stability of Saudi Arabia', *Middle East Report*, Vol. 21, No. 4, 1 July 1991.

Dunn, Michael Collins, 'Is the Sky Falling? Saudi Arabia's Economic Problems and Political Stability', *Middle East Policy*, Vol. III, No. 4, April 1995.

Economist Intelligence Unit, *Saudi Arabia Country Report*, 1st quarter, 1998.

Field, Michael, *Regional Development in Saudi Arabia: A Guide to Marketing, Trade Opportunities, Commercial Practice and Development in the Saudi Arabian Provinces,* Special Report prepared for COMET, London, May 1983.

'Filling a Void: A Survey of Saudi Arabia', *The Economist*, 13 February 1982.

Foreign and Commonwealth Office, Middle East Section. *Demography and Politics in the Middle East and North Africa*, Foreign Policy Document No. 202, April 1989.

Gause, Gregory F., 'The Gulf Conundrum: Economic Change, Population Growth, and Political Stability in the GCC States', *The Washington Quarterly*, Vol. 20, No. 1, Winter 1997.

Gause, Gregory F., *Oil Monarchies, Domestic and Security Challenges in the Arab Gulf States* (New York: Council on Foreign Relations Press, 1994).

The GCC Economic Databook, 1996.

Gerth, Jeff, 'Saudi Stability Hit by Heavy Spending Over Last Decade', *New York Times*, 22 August 1993.

Al-Ghayth, Muhammad Abdallah and Mansour Abdul-Aziz Al-Ma'shouq, ''Ard Mujaz li-Nata'ij Bahth: al-'Amala al-Muwatina fil-Qita' al-Ahli al-Saudi' ('National Employment in the Saudi Private Sector') *Al-Idara-l 'Amma Public Administration*, No. 82, March 1994.

Gresh, Alain, 'The Most Obscure Dictatorship', *Middle East Report*, Vol. 25, No. 197, 1 November 1995.

Hassanain, Khalid S. A., 'Saudi Mode of Greeting Rituals: Their Implications for Teaching and Learning English', *IRAL (International Review of Applied Linguistics in Language Teaching)*, Vol. XXXII, No. 1, February 1994.

Hegel, G.W.F., *Philosophy of Right* (translated with notes by T.M. Knox) in *Collected Works,* Vol. 3 (London/New York: Oxford University Press, 1967).

Henderson, Simon, *After King Fahd: Succession in Saudi Arabia*, Washington Institute Policy Paper No. 37 (Washington, DC: The Washington Institute for Near East Policy, 1994).

Hijab, N., *Woman Power: The Arab Debate on Women and Work* (Cambridge: Cambridge University Press, 1988).

Hobsbawm, E. and Terence Ranger (eds), *The Invention of Tradition* (Cambridge: Cambridge University Press, 1983).

Hunt, David Marshall and Mohammad I. Twaijri, 'Values and the Saudi Manager: An Empirical Investigation', *Journal of Management and Development*, Vol. 15, No. 5, 1996.

Jabbra, Nancy W. and Joseph G. Jabbra, 'Women and Development in the Middle East and North Africa', *Journal of Developing Societies*, Vol. VIII, 1992.

Jones, Clive, 'Saudi Arabia After the Gulf War: The International-External Security Dilemma', *International Relations*, Vol. 12, No. 6, 1995.

Kapstein, Nico, 'Materials for the History of the Prophet Muhammad's Birthday Celebration in Mecca', *Der Islam*, Vol. 69, No. 2, 1992.

Keane, John (ed.), *Civil Society and the State: New European Perspectives* (London/New York: Verso, 1988).

Kechichian, Joseph, 'Islamic Revivalism and the Change in Saudi Arabia: Juhayman-Al-Utaybi's "Letters" to the Saudi People', *The Muslim World*, Vol. LXXX, No. 1, January 1990.

Kemp, Peter, 'Saudi Arabia Ends the Uncertainty', *Middle East Economic Digest*, 12 January 1996.

Khalaf, Roula, 'The Shockwaves That Unsettle', *Financial Times*, 26 July 1996.

Konovsky, E., *The Economy of Saudi Arabia: Troubled Present, Grim Future*, Washington Institute Policy Paper No. 38 (Washington, DC: Washington Institute for Near East Policy, 1994).

Al-Kurdi, Muhammad Kamel Mustafa and Muhammad Abdallah al-Naji, 'Dirasa wa Tahlil Nuzum al-Qiyam al-Shakhsiyya lil-Mudir al-Saudi, fi Itar Madkhal Thaqafat-al-Munazamma' ('An Introduction to Institutional Culture: A Study and Analysis of Personal Ethics of Saudi Managers'), *Al-Idara-l 'Amma*, Vol. 36, No. 1, May 1996.

MacLeod, Arlene Elowe, *Accommodating Protest: Working Women, the New Veiling, and Change in Cairo* (New York: Columbia University Press, 1991).

Al-Manni', Mohammed A., 'Students' Perception of Academic Counselling at the King Saud University, Saudi Arabia', *International Review of Education*, Vol. 35, 1989.

Matthews, Roger and Mark Nicholson, 'Desert Kingdom's Flight of Fancy', *Financial Times*, 18 February 1994.

Middle East Economic Digest, 'Saudi Arabia's Private Sector Revival', 17 February 1989.

Middle East Executive Reports, Vol. 5, No. 5, 1982.

Ministry of Planning, Saudi Arabia, *Fifth Development Plan: 1990–1995*.

Mouffe, Chantal (ed.), *Gramsci and Marxist Theory* (London: Routledge and Kegan Paul, 1979).

NCB Economist, 'Gulf Population and Labour Force Structure', economic and financial publication issued by the Economics Department of the National Commercial Bank, Vol. 5, No. 4, June–July 1995.

Al-Nimr, Saud bin Muhammad, 'Ittijahat tullab al-Jami'ah Nahwa-l 'Amal fil-Qura wal-Aryaf bil-Mamlaka-l 'Arabiyya al-Saudiyya' ('Propensity for Saudi University Graduates to Seek Employment in Rural Areas of Saudi Arabia'), *Al-Idara-l 'Amma*, No. 73, March 1992.

Piscatori, James, *Islam in the Political Process* (Cambridge: RIIA/Cambridge University Press, 1983).

Popper, K., *The Open Society and its Enemies*, Vol. 2 in *The High Tide of Prophecy: Hegel, Marx and the Aftermath* (Princeton: Princeton University Press, 1963).

Pouillon, Francois, 'Un État Contre les Bédouins, l'Arabie Saoudite', *Monde Arabe Maghreb-Machrek*, No. 147, January–March 1995.

Al-Rasheed, Madawi, 'Saudi Arabia's Islamic Opposition', *Current History*, January 1996.

Al-Rasheed, Madawi and Loulouwa Al-Rasheed, 'The Politics of Encapsulation: Saudi Policy Towards Tribal and Religious Opposition', *Middle Eastern Studies*, Vol. 32, No. 1, January 1996.

Robinson, Bob, *The Saudi Labour Market: The Experience and Understanding of Saudi Development and Training Company* (Dammam: Saudi Development and Training Company Limited, July 1996).

Royal United Services Institute for Defence Studies, 'Report on Visit to Saudi Arabia: 27 October to 1 November 1990' (London: RUSI).

Rugh, William, 'The Emergence of a New Middle Class in Saudi Arabia', *Middle East Journal*, Vol. 27, No. 1, Winter 1973.

Al-Rumaihi, Mohammad, 'The Gulf Monarchies: Testing Time', *Middle East Quarterly*, Vol. 3, No. 4, December 1996.

El-Sanabary, Nagat, 'Women and the Nursing Profession in Saudi Arabia', in Suha Sabbagh (ed.), *Arab Women between Defiance and Restraint* (New York: Olive Branch Press, 1996).

'Saudia Arabia', *MEED Special Report*, Vol. 39, No. 10, 10 March 1995.

'Saudi Arabia', in 'The Postwar Gulf: New Business Realities in the Middle East', *Business International*, Report No. 2176, 1991.

'Saudi Arabia to Dig for Diversity', *International Herald Tribune*, 23 September 1996.

'Saudi Arabia's Future: The Cracks in the Kingdom', *The Economist*, 18 March 1995.

Saudi-British Bank, The HSBC Group Business Profile Series, *Saudi Arabia*, 6th edn, 3rd quarter, 1994.

'Saudi Security Forces are Capable of Pursuing Criminals', *MidEast Mirror*, Vol. 10, No. 215, 4 November 1996.

Simmons, Cyril and Christine Simmons, 'A Comparative Study of English and Muslim Adolescent Values', *Muslim Education Quarterly*, Vol. 12, No. 1, 1994.

Simmons, Cyril and Simmons, Christine, 'Personal and Moral Adolescent Values in England and Saudi Arabia', *Journal of Moral Education*, Vol. 23, No. 1, 1994, pp. 3–15.

Smith, Anthony, *National Identity* (London: Penguin, 1991).

Teitelbaum, Joshua, 'If You Can't Beat 'em, Buy 'em', Viewpoint, *The Jerusalem Report*, 16 November 1995.

'Telecoms: Region Joins the Global Revolution', *Middle East Economic Digest*, Vol. 40, No. 9, 1 March 1996.

Timewell, Stephen, 'Can the House of Saud Pay?', *The Banker*, September 1994.

Tocqueville, Alexis Charles de, *Democracy in America*, Vol. 2 (New York: Henri Maurice Clirel and J. & H.G. Langley, 1845).

Al-Tuwayjri, Muhammad bin Ibrahim, 'al-Ikhtilafat fis-tikhdam Uslubay Hal al-Mushkilat wa 'Ilqa' al-Lawm bayna-l 'Umala al-Wafida wal-'Umala-l Watiniyya' ('Differences in Problem Solving and Mutual Blame between Expatriate Workers and the Indigenous Workforce'), *Al-Idara-l 'Amma*, No. 71, July 1991.

US Department of State Report, March 1996.

World Bank, *World Tables, 1994* (Baltimore/London: Johns Hopkins University, 1994).

Yamani, Mai (ed.), *Feminism and Islam: Legal and Literary Perspectives* (London: Ithaca Press, 1996).

Yamani, Mai, 'Formality and Propriety in the Hijaz', unpublished PhD thesis, Oxford University, 1990.

Yamani, Mai, 'Health, Education, Gender and the Security of the Gulf in the Twenty-first Century', in David E. Long and Christian Koch (eds), *Gulf Security in the Twenty-first Century* (Abu Dhabi: The Emirates Centre for Strategic Studies and Research, 1997).

Yamani, Mai, 'Muslim Women and Human Rights: The New Generation in Saudi Arabia', in Eugene Cotran and Adel Sherif (eds), *Democracy, the Rule of Law and Islam* (London: Kluwer Law International, 1999).

Yamani, Mai, 'Saudi Arabia and Central Asia: The Islamic Connection', in Anoushiravan Ehteshami (ed.), *From the Gulf to Central Asia: Players in the New Great Game* (Exeter: University of Exeter Press, 1994).

Yaphe, Judith, S., 'Saudi Arabia: Uncertain Stability', *Strategic Forum*, No. 125, July 1997.